Gateways
to GOD

Gateways to GOD

Celebrating the Sacraments

Fr. Robert J. Hater

Our Sunday Visitor Publishing Division
Our Sunday Visitor, Inc.
Huntington, Indiana 46750

Nihil Obstat
Msgr. Michael Heintz, Ph.D.
Censor Librorum

Imprimatur
☩ Kevin C. Rhoades
Bishop of Fort Wayne-South Bend
August 8, 2011

The *Nihil Obstat* and *Imprimatur* are official declarations that a book is free from doctrinal or moral error. It is not implied that those who have granted the *Nihil Obstat* and *Imprimatur* agree with the contents, opinions, or statements expressed.

ISBN: 978-1-59276-826-4 (Inventory No. T1129)
LCCN: 2011930586

Cover design: Rebecca J. Heaston
Cover photo: Shutterstock
Interior design: Dianne Nelson

PRINTED IN THE UNITED STATES OF AMERICA

DEDICATION

This year is the fifty-second anniversary of my ordination to the priesthood. I thank my parents for giving my sisters, my brother, and me a wonderful home and a good education. In a simple and unassuming way, they imitated Christ as people for others. I dedicate this book to them for their love and to my entire family for their friendship.

TABLE OF CONTENTS

ACKNOWLEDGMENTS

I AM GRATEFUL to those who advised me in writing this book. I thank Bert Ghezzi, acquisitions editor at Our Sunday Visitor. He invited me to write the book, suggested the topic of sacraments, and assisted me with his professional advice.

I also thank the following persons for reading the manuscript and giving me excellent suggestions: Rev. Jeffrey M. Kemper, Rev. Giles H. Pater, Sister Jeanette Jabour, O.P., Joan Kohl, Amy Spessard, Julie St. Croix, and Ruth Trentman.

I especially thank Julie St. Croix for her comments that made a significant difference in the revised book. I appreciated her contributions all the more, for shortly before I sent her the manuscript, her father, Paul Underwood, suddenly died. When returning home from his funeral in Canada, Julie critiqued the book. I express my sincerest sympathy to her and her family. May her father, Paul, rest in peace, and may the entire Underwood family be blessed with the memory of his good life and his eternal blessedness with God.

༄

INTRODUCTION

CAN THIS WORLD EVER BRING TRUE HAPPINESS?

What kind of success makes us happy?

It can't be money or accomplishments. They soon fade away. Scripture says that the key to genuine happiness rests in God. Those who believe in God and accept Jesus as Lord are the really happy ones, for they know what it means to be truly loved.

I always felt this way. I never remember a time when I didn't feel loved. Even when feeling sick and rejected, an inner force drives me to know that somewhere, somehow, I am loved. The root of this feeling is deeper than the solid foundation for love coming from my parents and family in early life. It goes beyond the love shown by my friends. Their love, however, points to a deeper source of love, who is God.

God's love comes through the sacramentality of life itself. Upon it rests the sacramentality of the Church and the seven sacraments.

God calls us to follow him, as he called Abraham, Moses, Rebecca, Mary, Peter, and other biblical figures. Jesus said, "You did not choose me but I chose you" (Jn 15:16). To follow Jesus requires taking up our cross. On our journey, Jesus offers us the gift of faith.

Because of original sin, the world is strongly influenced by evil. It tempts us to forget God and make gods of earthly things. This struggle between right and wrong has existed since Adam and Eve said no to God.

God knows that our struggle is not easy, and he promises to remain with us. We first experience his presence in nature, for creation opens us up to God's wonders and the blessings of eternity.

Knowledge of God comes through creation. Appreciating this helps us see how nature's beauty reflects God's beauty and how God's presence in nature connects with God's revelation in Jesus, the Church, and the sacraments.

All nature prepares us to accept God's love. We see glimpses of it everywhere. I saw it on my yearly retreat as I walked alone over a farm field. Suddenly a baby buck bolted from the weeds nearby. It jumped and leaped; its spindly legs hardly able to sustain its weight. This recently born buck played joyfully, as it bounded over a fence and disappeared. The next day, I saw it again with its twin sister, an equally fragile doe. The little buck never stopped running and prancing, while his sister grazed quietly in the weeds. I watched, aware that coyotes live in the vicinity. "The mother doe," I thought, "must be nearby." Sure enough, as I glanced toward the corner of the field, a large doe stood there, patiently guarding the small buck and doe. She never moved. If danger approached, her signal would call them, and if necessary she would defend them with her life.

The mother deer's love reminded me of God's ever-present love. God knows our needs and shares his love with those who ask. To show his love, God gave us Jesus, who, in turn, gave us the sacraments as special signs of this love.

Jesus is our prime gateway to happiness. He stays with us in joy and sorrow. He invites us to meet him as he assists us in the sacraments. Each sacrament manifests this love and connects us to Jesus' death and resurrection.

The more we grow to recognize Jesus' love, the better we know why he gave us the sacraments as signs of God's abiding love. The more we know about the sacraments, the better we appreciate them. The better we appreciate them, the more we recognize the depths of God's love.

The sacraments mirror God's divine love. Just as he set the rainbow in the heavens to pledge his fidelity to the Chosen People in the Old Testament, so also Jesus gave us the sacraments, especially the Eucharist, to pledge his love. Through them, we celebrate our "Amen" to the Father's love, thank Jesus for redeeming us, and profess our belief in the Holy Spirit's abiding presence in the Church.

Just as Jesus is our gateway to happiness, the sacraments are also gateways. A gateway always leads to something else. For instance, life's sacramentality is the gateway to God and to divine revelation in the Old and New Testaments. Jesus is the gateway to salvation, and the Church is the gateway to the kingdom of God and the sacraments. Seen in this way, the sacraments link up with the sacramentality manifested in our love for a child, the beauty of a sunset, the power of the ocean, and the wonders of the universe.

Chapter One of this book looks at the world's sacramentality as a gateway to appreciating Jesus as a sacrament, the Church as a sacrament, and the seven sacraments in general. Chapter Two considers Baptism as the gateway to eternal life, the foundation for a life of grace, and membership in the Church. Chapter Three describes how Confirmation leads us to a deeper union with the Holy Spirit and the Church. Chapter Four considers the Eucharist as the gateway to a deeper celebration of God's love and the mystery of Jesus' passion, death, resurrection, and ascension. Chapter Five reflects on Reconciliation as leading us to the healing of our soul, union with God, and conversion. Chapter Six studies how the Anointing of the Sick can lead us to renewed health here and eternal life hereafter. Chapter Seven considers Matrimony as the way to affirm the body's sacramental nature and God's love, reflected in spousal love. Chapter Eight analyzes Holy Orders as the key to a deeper incorporation into the priesthood of Jesus Christ.

Each chapter concludes with "Communal and Personal Implications."

CHAPTER ONE

࿇

Life, Sacramentality, and the Sacraments

The World, Jesus, the Church, and the Sacraments as Gateways to God

IN THE SECOND YEAR OF MY DOCTORAL WORK, the pressures built up, and I needed to get away. One afternoon, I drove to Rockaway Beach, New York, near Coney Island. I arrived just as the sunlight faded on the water. The increased sound of surf on the shore calmed me.

I sat alone and then walked along the beach for hours. I was a solitary figure with a strong sense that a powerful force overtook my body. As I walked, I don't know if I saw anyone or not. I only remember the overpowering awareness that someone greater than I walked with me. I felt very small as I experienced the pounding waves that brought a soothing feeling. As the last rays of sunlight disappeared, I felt this strong force beyond me in the evening beauty and the sky's magnificent colors.

As night descended, I stood alone on the beach, except for my feeling of God's presence, which turned my stress into solitude and my fears into hope. God's love, peace, patience, and hope came through creation.

What made this possible? A spark of divinity, present within me, came to life through my flesh and bones. From that evening onward, I found this same God everywhere, even in God's apparent absence. Forty years later, this same spark of divinity continues to pulsate through the gateway of my body. I still experience the all-good and wise God around, within, inside, and beyond me.

God's presence as I experienced it on Rockaway Beach is available to all of us in one form or another. The world where we live and work is the first place where we experience God. It comes through our children, who reflect God's presence. A husband and wife's love and a friend's warmth manifest God's presence in loving relationships. According to Pope John Paul II, God inscribes into our bodies the language of love that points to the mystery of Trinitarian love.[1] God selflessly shares this love with us, a love fully revealed in Jesus' life, death, and resurrection. We appreciate this gift of love because we are sacramental beings.

This gift of God's love makes human love possible. God's love is more profound than the mystery revealed by the waves breaking on the shore or the grandeur of the last slivers of light descending over the ocean. The awe and wonder, experienced in human love, helps us appreciate that we are sacramental.

We reflect God's love by loving our spouses and children. Spousal love manifests God's love. There is no better way for children to learn God's love than through loving parents. We are God's gateways to Trinitarian love. Our bodies contain the blueprint that discloses God to us. We need to pay attention to them as gateways that provide the key to God's love.

The *Catechism of the Catholic Church* begins the treatment of the sacraments by describing the role of the Trinity in God's plan for salvation. It says that "the Father accomplishes the 'mystery of his will' by giving his beloved Son and his Holy Spirit for the salvation of the world and for the glory of his name (Eph 1:9)" (CCC 1066). All the persons of the Trinity play a part in our salvation.

Gateways, Sacramentality, and the Sacraments

Alone among earthly creatures, we can ask about God and reflect on who we are, why we are here, and where we are going. We can know, love, and serve God, not as disembodied spirits but as individuals with a body and a soul, who rely on the sacramental nature of life as a gateway to God.

As implied in the Introduction, a "gateway" is something we pass through to get somewhere else.

We pass through the gateway of a sports stadium to cheer on our team. We enter an office through a gateway. We go into our parish church through a gateway. At life's end, we pass into heaven through a gateway. The world, Jesus, the Church, and the seven sacraments are gateways to God.

What is a sacrament and what are the seven sacraments of the Catholic Church? The early Latin Church chose the Latin word *sacramentum* to replace the original Greek word *mysterion*, used for the celebration of God's love, revealed in the Paschal Mystery. Eastern Catholic Churches still refer to sacraments as *mysteries*.

The Latin word *sacramentum* refers to the pledge of faithfulness taken by a Roman soldier entering military service. This pledge committed him to loyalty and a new life. It was a gateway. In a similar way, the sacraments are gateways, opening us up to a new life in Christ. They celebrate Jesus' Paschal Mystery and God's promise of eternal life.

The *Catechism of the Catholic Church* defines the sacraments as "efficacious signs of grace, instituted by Christ and entrusted to the Church, by which divine life is dispensed to us" (CCC 1131). (Here, "efficacious" means that the sacraments bring about God's grace in us.) This resembles the definition from the *Baltimore Catechism*, once popular with Catholics, namely, "A sacrament is an outward sign instituted by Christ to give grace."[2]

God created this sacramental universe according to divine designs. Genesis says, "In the beginning, when God created the heavens and the earth, the earth was a formless void . . ." (Gen 1:1). God created "living creatures of every kind" (Gen 1:24) and made man and woman "in his image" (Gen 1:27). Although a near infinity of creatures exists, all originate in and manifest God. They are one in their purpose of serving the Creator's designs, one in their basic goodness, and one in their ability to disclose God.

All creation reflects God and God-like qualities, such as love, goodness, and truth. Psalm 19 says, "The heavens are telling the glory of God; / and the firmament proclaims his handiwork. / Day to day pours forth speech, / and night to night declares knowledge" (Ps 19:1-2).

Water can symbolize life or death. We need water's life-giving qualities to survive and thrive, but a hurricane or flood shows water's destructive power. The Church uses water's life-and-death symbolism in Baptism. Through it, we die to our old ways of sin and are born into Jesus' new life of grace.

Bread symbolizes our need for nourishment. At the Last Supper, Jesus transformed bread into his body and wine into his blood. He told us that these are necessary for our spiritual survival.

The world reveals God's existence and gives us clues about God, but not in the same way that Scripture, Jesus, and the Church reveal God. Nature tells us that there is a God. Scripture and Sacred Tradition tell us more. They reveal God's plan of salvation and help us appreciate how Jesus redeems the human race through his death and resurrection. The Church safeguards God's Revelation from error, and the seven sacraments celebrate the world, redeemed by God's love.

Our body is the gateway to the sacramental world. It links the natural and the spiritual. In passing through this gateway, we find God in created realities, as we discover goodness in nature and other persons.

The World as the Initial Gateway to Eternal Life

Pope John Paul II says, "The body, and it alone, is capable of making visible what is invisible: the spiritual and the divine. It was created to transfer into the visible reality of the world the mystery hidden since time immemorial in God, and thus be a sign of it."[3]

I experienced a revelation of God's presence in my relationship with my father when he was dying.

Holding my dad's hand in the hospital room became a vehicle of God-centered love. His hand was frail and blotched, resulting from months of lying on his back and enduring the numerous intravenous devices put into his arms and hands. Grasping the tissue — the thin skin of his hands and arms was symbolic of my finitude and God's mysterious ways — I sensed God's deep and abiding presence with Dad as life ebbed from his bones.

I realized how love between two people discloses the presence of a love that goes beyond either of them. I felt God's love coming through our love. This God-centered awareness was simple, yet profound. Dad reflected God to me. I found God in our mutual love. Day after day, as we sat together, my dad was a treasure and a holy manifestation of God.

Dad's frail body was a gateway to someone beyond him. God connects to us through the human body. Our bodies reflect the blueprint of the divine and are gateways to the sacramental world. The body invites us to enter God's world. As Pope John Paul II says, "So in man created in the image of God there was revealed, in a way, the very sacramentality of creation, the sacramentality of the world. Man, in fact, by means of his corporality, his masculinity and femininity, becomes a visible sign of the economy of truth and love, which has its source in God himself and which was revealed already in the mystery of creation."[4]

When reflecting on love, knowledge, or anything else, I realize that everything about me comes through my body. None of my thoughts, feelings, or actions is independent of my body. I cannot know Jesus or the Church in isolation from my body. The body filters all my experiences.

But my body is more. It is a sacred sign, or sacrament, revealing God. This revelatory process began when I first came from my mother's womb. This was based on my relationships with her, Dad, and others who communicated God's love through their love. They introduced and fostered my growth. At the same time, something else took root within me. It was the new life — the eternal life — into which the gateway of Baptism initiated me. As I matured, I learned that Jesus and the Church are gateways to the kingdom and to eternal life. On every level, my body is the conduit that reveals the mystery of eternal life.

The body establishes the fundamental orientation allowing only humans to appreciate the world's sacramentality as a path to God.

The human quest for God takes different forms, but each begins with our need to question and wonder why. When children begin to speak, one of their first questions is "Why?" In the earliest years, we reach beyond ourselves and search for more to fulfill the built-in yearning to discover life's meaning. This yearning is contained in the blueprint of our bodies.

As we mature, our questioning becomes more sophisticated. We ask about life's purpose and destiny, and we look for answers in creation, people, books, the Internet, and inner reflection. This search continues into adulthood. The answers we receive push us beyond ourselves, as we recognize more in nature than what first appears.

We see more in a flower than a flower; we see a reflection of God. We find more in a hurricane than a hurricane; we find the mystery of death and destruction. We live, work, worry, celebrate, love, and fear, and we wonder "Why?" We do this because our body is sacramental and connects us with God.

Made in God's image, we recognize God's presence in the world, but this awareness isn't always clear. Original sin dims our minds and wounds our nature, but not to the extent that we are unable to know God through creation. The body's blueprint for knowing God is connected with our need to search for God.

We must question to fulfill our eternal destiny. We ask, "Who am I? Why am I here? Why is there suffering? What happens after death?" When we look to creation for answers, often we are not satisfied because God's creation is limited in its ability to help us address such questions. The only adequate answers come from God's divine revelation in the Old and New Testaments. Here, we learn that God creates us to live forever and that Jesus shows us the way. He brings hope, confidence, and trust in both good and difficult times, reflected in the following episode.

It was Good Friday, and our family thought Mom would die between one and three in the afternoon. She didn't. Finally, about 6:30 p.m., I left her room to get something to eat. I had been with her for the better part of the past thirty-six hours, and I was exhausted.

After forty-five minutes, I returned. Walking back into the hospital room, I immediately realized that Mom was dead. Two nurses were at her side, and a friend was next to her. I fell to my knees by her bedside. Holding her hand, I sobbed and sobbed. I thought of Mary, Jesus' mother, holding the hand and body of Jesus. God seemed distant at that moment, as I became one with Mary as she held Jesus.

A hollow feeling filled me and I asked, "Why? Why so much suffering? Why so much tragedy? Why so much death?" No answers came that evening; only the realization that somehow, someday, resurrection would happen for me, as it already happened for my mother.

Without joy, I still was hopeful. Hope allowed me to break through this devastating time. It allowed me to connect with the transcendent God who was with me on Rockaway Beach and who was with me also after Mom's death. When Mom died, I found God, not in an overpowering awareness of divine presence but in the solitude of God's absence.

Put simply, made in God's image, humans alone embody the one God shining through creation. Our bodies manifest God's truth and love. Because our sacramentality reveals God, we can share God's love with others.

Jesus, the Church, and the Seven Sacraments

The world's sacramentality is the gateway to the supernatural life. We better appreciate the God beyond us by experiencing the God with us. I grow in awareness of God's mystery every time I enter the woods at my Indiana home.

I've walked this land for over forty years. Each time I sit by the lake, struggle through the underbrush, or walk down a well-manicured trail, I am struck by a new miracle of nature. I see fish jumping out of the water in their quest for bugs. I see small wild flowers, more dainty than any plant sold in stores. I see beautiful and tragic episodes, like a deer impaled on a fence. Each scene reminds me that there is more to life than what seems apparent.

Once, I walked along a back trail through ten inches of snow, admiring the multiple footprints of birds, small rodents, and large animals that traversed the same ground since the last snowfall two days earlier. I also noticed small drops of blood, every three or four feet apart.

Did the blood come from a smaller animal killed by a larger one, or was it the blood of an animal, freshly injured in the woods and trying to get home? I'll never know, but the blood spattering reminded me of life's struggles, that all existence is suffused with life and death.

The blood in the snow symbolized the multiple mysteries evident on the land as plants, animals, and humans live and die. It reminded me, too, of the trail of blood left in the dusty sand on a hill in Jerusalem, as Jesus dragged his cross to Calvary. It reminded me of the price that he paid for our salvation and how his death and resurrection climaxes all earthly struggles.

The blood on the snow was a sacred sign of God's love for all humankind.

Jesus is the most perfect revelation of God. Because he is the Son of God, we can learn about God by reflecting on Jesus' life, ministry, and teachings. Jesus is a sign, or sacred symbol, reflecting God. As such, he is a sacrament, and in fact, the most perfect and sublime sacrament.

This is clearly seen in the Gospel on the feast of the Transfiguration. Pope St. Leo the Great commented on it, saying, "The Lord reveals his glory in the presence of chosen witnesses. His body is like that of the rest of mankind, but he makes it shine with such splendor that his face becomes like the sun in glory, and his garments as white as snow."[5]

Jesus' body is a sacrament, or holy sign, as he appears with Moses and Elijah in the Gospel. This event anticipates his resurrection and continued presence among us on earth through his glorified body.

He is the most perfect sacrament, revealing the Trinity. Not long before he went to Jerusalem to suffer and die, he said: "Whoever has seen me has seen the Father" (Jn 14:9). Jesus is forever, the all-embracing sacrament, revealing God to us (CCC 1088-1090).

This would not have been possible if the divine Son of God hadn't assumed a human body. The joining of divinity and humanity in Christ forever glorifies the human body, wounded by Adam's sin. Sanctified by Jesus, our human bodies become sacred temples of God. As Jesus says, "We will come . . . and make our home with them" (Jn 14:23). The Trinity lives within us and invites us to work out our salvation by cooperating with God's grace.

St. Leo the Great continues, "With no less forethought [Jesus] was also providing a firm foundation for the hope of holy Church. The whole body of Christ was to understand the kind of transformation that it would receive as his gift. The members of that body were to look forward to a share in that glory which first blazed out in Christ their head."[6]

These words reflect the connection between Jesus and the Church, his Mystical Body. As with Jesus, there is more to the Church than what first appears. As Jesus is more than a man who walked the earth, being the Son of God, so the Church is more than an effective religious organization existing throughout the ages, being a sign of God's abiding presence.

Jesus is the sacrament *par excellence.* His Mystical Body is the most eminent sacrament, or sign, of God's abiding presence on earth. The *Catechism of the Catholic Church* says, "As sacrament, the Church is Christ's instrument. 'She is . . . the universal sacrament of salvation' " (CCC 776).

Jesus is the gateway leading Church members to salvation through the inspiration of the Holy Spirit. The Trinity communicates with us through the sacramentality of the Church.

As we have seen, all creation manifests God. We know, feel, and worship through our bodies, Jesus, and the Church. The seven sacraments celebrate life's joys, happiness, suffering, and death. They put us on the way to God's kingdom, thus preparing us for eternal life.

Divine actions, closely associated with Jesus' death and resurrection, are at the root of all the sacraments. Through them, Jesus reveals the saving message of his Paschal Mystery (his Passion, death, resurrection, and ascension) and invites us to share in the life of the Church.

The sacraments confer the graces that they signify on those receiving them. We call these graces by the terms "sanctifying grace," "actual grace," and "sacramental grace." Sanctifying grace (or habitual grace) is the grace of divine friendship, the new life of God, which makes a person a son or daughter of God. When we are in a relationship of friendship and have not cut ourselves off from God through serious, or mortal, sin, we are in the state of sanctifying grace. Actual graces are divine helps given in the sacraments and at other times. For example, if a person has difficulty dealing with a vice, like anger, the sacrament of Reconciliation provides special graces to help deal with it. If a woman needs confidence and spiritual help when interviewing for a nursing job, the Eucharist is a wonderful time to ask for such help. We can ask for God's help or actual graces at any time or any place, whenever we have difficulties at home, problems with neighbors, or challenges at work. Sacramental graces are actual graces of the Holy Spirit, special to the particular sacrament, which Christ confers on the one receiving it. For instance, the sacramental graces of Matrimony help a couple to fulfill their responsibilities in married life, and the sacramental graces of Holy Orders help the ordained minister to be faithful to his calling. Sacramental graces are particularly helpful during transition times, like birth, marriage, and retirement. Such transitions need to be celebrated by rites of passage.

All cultures recognize this need. A custom in one particular Chinese group tells the people that birth does not complete a baby's entrance into life. The baby is not considered fully human until it undergoes the ritual of "Passing through the Gate." In this ritual, the gate is a large one, made of bamboo.

Not long after a child's birth, the parents — accompanied by the child, family, and friends — pass ritualistically through the gate, which symbolizes life. Only when the child and family pass through it, and the child ritualistically enters the community, does the group consider the child as ready to live.

The Chinese developed their ritual to celebrate the beginning of the child's life. Jesus established the seven sacraments to help us celebrate transition times all along life's journey. Presupposing life's sacramentality, they play a vital role in such transitions.

Sacraments open up new challenges and opportunities on our journey to the kingdom of God. The remainder of this book treats each sacrament as a gateway that celebrates a life transition. These chapters presume welcome and hospitality. They rest on foundations set by the sacraments of initiation. The sacraments are rooted in God himself, who invites us to be born anew into his divine life through Baptism, who strengthens us in the sacrament of Confirmation, and who gives us the food for everlasting life in the Eucharist (CCC 1212).

☙

COMMUNAL AND PERSONAL IMPLICATIONS

What implications can we draw from this chapter for Christian living in our family, neighborhood, work, and church?

When I reflect on this question, I remember our family's frequent picnics in the Cincinnati parks. From them, I developed a greater closeness to my parents and siblings, as well as a love for nature, sports, and cooking out. It wasn't what we did, but that we did it together and enjoyed the outdoors as a manifestation of God's beauty. To these picnics, I attribute my initial awareness of how God's presence in creation connects with Jesus' presence in my life.

In a simple way, my parents taught us how the things we learned in books and from people linked with a bigger world where God lives. From early childhood, I learned about the sacramentality of the world and how it set the stage for sacramentality in the Church. My parents, in their wisdom, made life the stage where God dwells and is revealed.

We can develop a similar awareness in today's children, often caught up in the world of iPods, cell phones, the Internet, sports, and television. For this to happen, we must acknowledge God's presence in the broader world.

We don't have to take long walks in nature or go on creation-centered vacations to find God. We can simply look into the eyes of our children and loved ones, for we cannot meditate on the wonder of the human body for long without appreciating the God who created us. As our recognition of Jesus grows and we learn more about him, it becomes harder to hurt others and harbor grudges.

As we consider others, let's not forget ourselves. Wisdom leads us to probe the depths of our soul and become more aware of God, who dwells there. In so doing, we remember that Jesus promised to be with us until the end of time and to send the Holy Spirit to dwell with us. We recall the Trinity's presence as we pray to the Father, the Son, and the Holy Spirit:

- How does nature lead us to God and show us that creation alone is not sufficient to answer life's mysteries?
- How does nature open us up to see the need for further revelation from God in Scripture and the Church's Tradition?
- What has happened in your life that showed you the world's sacramentality?
- Knowing that the body alone is capable of making visible the spiritual and the divine, what is your attitude toward your body?
- Give examples of how life is a gift from God.
- Our bodies are blueprints of God's truth and love. What does this tell us about the casual attitude of many people toward sex?
- Our ability to know God's mystery is conditioned by the degree to which we search for God. What does this imply about the importance of prayer?
- The only adequate answers to life's deep questions come from God's divine Revelation in the Old and New Testaments, where we learn that God created us to live forever. What does this tell us about our present attitude toward knowing more about our faith?
- The seven sacraments are gateways to joy, happiness, suffering, and death in

this life, and these prepare us for eternal life. What are the implications of this for your life?

- How does the world's sacramentality lead you to Christ, and how does Jesus, the most perfect sacrament, reveal the Trinity to you? What does this mean? How does it indicate the importance of developing our relationship with Jesus through prayer?

- Our need to share love with children, spouses, parents, friends, and others points to a greater need for love, found only in God. What does this tell us about human dignity and the need to reach out and support others as temples of the Holy Spirit? What does this say about the sacramentality of the Church?

- Each life transition — birth, marriage, suffering, and death, for example — challenges us to continue on life's journey in a healthy way. What does this tell us about the need to ritualize such transitions through the sacraments?

ॐ

CHAPTER TWO

Baptism

Gateway to Eternal Life, the Foundation for a Life of Grace, and Membership in the Church

MARCO WAS THREE WEEKS OLD when I first met him and Lucy, his mother. When Lucy brought Marco into the room, her countenance beamed, as she looked lovingly into her first child's face. She said, "Isn't he an angel!" while moving him closer to me. I nodded. We spoke of Marco's baptism and how wonderful it would be. I told her that it was the initial gateway into Marco's new life in Christ.

I said, "Marco is beautiful because he is made in God's image. You and your husband will help him grow in God's love. You cannot do this alone, for Marco needs God's special help, promised by Jesus, who told his disciples that we must be born again to be saved. The new life that Marco receives at Baptism is God's own life." Lucy smiled and replied, "I am eager to do my part to see that Marco appreciates this new life in Christ when he is older."

Baptism opens up new possibilities to us. Just as opening the gates of a football arena allows us to enter and see a sporting event or opening doors of a theater allows us to see a movie, God opened the gates to eternal happiness, which were closed through Adam's sin. Through Jesus' dying and rising, God gives us a free ticket to enter these gates through Baptism.

Being born again is God's free gift, given at Baptism. It provides access to other gifts bestowed through the other sacraments.

Baptism as an Initial Gateway

The *Catechism of the Catholic Church* indicates that from apostolic times, becoming a Christian involves a journey that includes several stages. This journey can take place gradually or quickly, but certain essential elements must be present. These include the need for (a) proclaiming God's Word by Christian disciples, (b) accepting that Word in faith, (c) making a profession of faith, and (d) being baptized. When all this happens through the power of the Holy Spirit, the person of faith enters into an ongoing conversion process and has the right to receive the Eucharist as a member of the Church, Christ's Eucharistic people (CCC 1229).

The *Catechism* also says, "Holy Baptism is the basis of the whole Christian life, the gateway to life in the Spirit (*vitae spiritualis ianua*), and the door which gives access to the other sacraments" (CCC 1213). Baptism takes away original sin and forgives personal sins, gives us new birth as sons and daughters of God, makes us members of Christ and his Church, encourages us to be persons for others, and gives us a share in the priesthood of Jesus Christ.

The Greek word for Baptism, *baptizein*, means to plunge or immerse. The symbolism of being plunged or immersed into baptismal waters indicates that we die to the old ways of sin and death, are buried with Christ, and are raised up to a new life with the Lord. At our baptism, we are reborn through water and the Holy Spirit, and we are enlightened in God's ways.

Baptism is our initial gateway to heaven. This blessed state is anticipated on earth and fulfilled in the afterlife. For Christians, reborn into the life of Christ, eternal life has already begun. The *Rite of Baptism for Children* says, "[Y]ou have become a new creation, and have clothed yourself in Christ . . ." (n. 99). Reflecting this theme, the priest or deacon concludes this ritual by blessing everyone, saying:

> **Celebrant:** By God's gift, through water and the Holy Spirit, we are reborn to everlasting life. In his goodness, may he continue to pour out his blessings upon these sons and daughters of his. May he make them always, wherever they may be, faithful members of his holy people. May he send his peace upon

all who are gathered here, in Christ Jesus our
Lord.
All: Amen. (*Rite of Baptism for Children* 105)

History of Baptism

Christian Baptism is prefigured in the Old Testament.
During the blessing of baptismal water at the Easter
Vigil liturgy, Scripture tells us that when creation be-
gan, God's Spirit swept over the waters (cf. Gen 1:2 and
Easter Vigil reading from the *Roman Missal*).

When the priest blesses the baptismal water at
the Easter Vigil, the Church recalls certain events of
Israelite history that prefigured Baptism. At the beginning of creation, water provided a source of nourishment and fruitfulness. Genesis 1:2 speaks of the
waters of creation, ". . . a wind from God swept over
the face of the waters." These waters, gushing from
the earth, represent life and prefigure the cleansing
waters of Baptism.

The Easter Vigil liturgy also represents Noah's
ark as prefiguring the salvation brought by Baptism.
The *Catechism of the Catholic Church* adds, "If water springing up from the earth symbolizes life, the
water of the sea is a symbol of death and so can represent the mystery of the cross. By this symbolism
Baptism signifies communion with Christ's death"
(CCC 1220).

In addition, the Easter Vigil liturgy tells us that the crossing of the Red Sea, whereby the Jews were freed from the oppression of the Egyptians, prefigures the liberation from sin that happens at Baptism. The subsequent crossing of the Jordan River, enabling the Jews to take possession of the land promised to their ancestor Abraham, anticipates our entrance into eternal life.

Jesus fulfills these prophetic episodes. His public life begins with John's baptism, a prelude to Jesus giving us new life through water and the Holy Spirit. Jesus accomplished this by his death, resurrection, ascension, and sending the Holy Spirit on Pentecost. After the Resurrection, Jesus commanded his followers to make disciples of all nations and to baptize them in the name of the Father, and of the Son, and of the Holy Spirit (Mt 28:19).

The New Testament contains many references to Baptism. From Pentecost on, the Church fulfilled Jesus' command to baptize and spread his message through the world. The Great Commission of Jesus (Mt 28) — to go forth and make disciples of all nations, and to baptize them in the name of the Father, and of the Son, and of the Holy Spirit — implies that the Gospel is to be preached and accepted in faith before the new believers are baptized. To all indications, this was borne out in baptismal practice.

Everywhere the apostles and disciples went, they preached Jesus' message and baptized believers. Although they baptized in various languages and

rites, this sacrament remained the same at its core
— namely, those receiving it were born into the new
life of Christ through the power of the Holy Spirit.

During early persecution, the Church met se-
cretly, administered the sacraments, and developed
a rite of initiation into the Christian community.
This included the present-day sacraments of Baptism, Confirmation, and the Eucharist. The Church
celebrated this rite until persecution ended, and
Christianity spread freely. During persecution,
some catechumens suffered martyrdom (Baptism of
blood) rather than deny their faith.

Early Church history gives evidence that adults
and children were baptized. It makes sense that
when an entire household came into the Church, it
was naturally the desire of parents that their children
were also baptized. The Catholic tradition has assumed that baptism of the jailer and his entire family, mentioned in Acts 16:25-34, included the baptism
of his young children. The practice of infant Baptism
was clearly established by the time of St. Augustine
in northern Africa (fourth and fifth centuries), because he points to it as an indication of the Church's
belief in original sin.

In the Latin (Western) Catholic Church, as conver-
sions became more numerous, it was difficult for the
bishop to preside over all of them. Hence, priests in
local areas started baptizing adult converts and children, while the bishop restricted the administration of
Confirmation to himself. In this way, the bishop kept

contact with his people, even if it meant putting off their Confirmation until years after their baptism.

Hence, the Latin Church separated Baptism from Confirmation. As time went on, some Catholics never were confirmed, and others received the Eucharist before Confirmation. Eventually, baptism of children became the norm in the Latin Church and the ancient rite of initiation of adults ended. The changed order of Baptism, the Eucharist, and finally Confirmation remained the commonly accepted practice in the Latin Catholic Church.

The Eastern Catholic Churches have maintained the unity between the three sacraments of initiation. Eastern bishops and priests administered them in one rite, even after the number of converts multiplied. This custom still survives, even with infants.

Throughout the Middle Ages, Baptism remained separated from the other sacraments of initiation in the Latin Catholic Church.

As the centuries progressed, the relationship between grace and Baptism was clarified. This was, in part, due to St. Thomas Aquinas' theological perspectives on grace and the developing terminology that addressed the mystery of grace and free will.

As this was happening, the Councils of Lyons (1274), Florence (1439), and Trent (1545-1563) defined that there are seven sacraments. To counter the threats from the Protestant Reformation, the Council of Trent clarified the Church's teachings on the seven sacraments.

The Second Vatican Council (1962-1965) decreed that a *Rite of Christian Initiation of Adults* (RCIA) be reestablished for the Latin Church, akin to the ancient rites of Christian initiation. The RCIA incorporates elements of the conversion process of an adult coming to faith and living by faith. These include:

- The **Period of Evangelization and the Precatechumenate** begins with the inquirer reflecting on whether to begin the RCIA process, which leads to Baptism and entrance into the Church. This involves deciding to inquire about beginning the process and approaching a parish. This begins a time of initial evangelization (learning more about the faith) within the parish community.

  The First Step is being accepted into the order of the Catechumens.

- The **Period of the Catechumens** follows. It is the time when the catechumen is catechized, deepens faith, decides to be baptized, and is accepted by the Church (elected) to receive the sacraments of initiation.

  The Second Step is election and the enrollment of names.

- This is followed by the **Period of Purification and Enlightenment**. It is the time when the catechumen enters into immediate preparation for Baptism, thus experiencing purification and enlightenment.

*The Third Step is the celebration of the sacra-
ments of initiation, which includes being baptized, anointed (confirmed), and welcomed to the
Eucharistic table.*

• The **Period of Postbaptismal Catechesis
(Mystagogy)** concludes the process. It lasts
through the entire Easter season and is the time
when the neophyte (newly baptized person)
deepens his or her incorporation into the Church
after celebrating the sacraments of initiation.

*Ongoing faith formation continues throughout a
person's entire life.*

Throughout this entire process of coming to
faith and living by faith, the biblical Word of God
plays a vital role in hearing Jesus' Gospel, changing
one's life, and living according to an awakened, instructed conscience. Reflecting on the Scriptures —
often the Sunday readings — and praying with them
are a vital part of the RCIA process.

This rite began to be practiced in the 1970s. Today, it is the ordinary way to bring converts into the
Latin Catholic Church, as it stresses the close relationship between Baptism and the Eucharist. The
Church incorporated this closeness into the new
rites for the administration of Baptism. In both the
Eastern and Latin Catholic Churches, Baptism is a
perpetual symbol of God's love, offering the promise
of eternal life.

Basic Church Teachings on Baptism

The *Catechism of the Catholic Church* says, "Baptism is necessary for salvation for those to whom the Gospel has been proclaimed and who have had the possibility of asking for this sacrament" (CCC 1257). This harkens back to Jesus' words, "Very truly, I tell you, no one can enter the kingdom of God without being born of water and Spirit" (Jn 3:5). If God gives us faith and the knowledge of the Son of God, we must accept God's invitation to be baptized, for it is the gateway to eternal life.

Those who, before receiving Baptism, give up their lives for the faith in martyrdom, in imitation of Christ, can be saved through Baptism of blood. Something similar applies to unbaptized people who die before Baptism, not yet having received water Baptism or Baptism of blood. They, too, can be saved if they consciously desired Baptism, would have explicitly desired it if they knew of its necessity for salvation, or sought the truth according to their faith, while ignorant of the Gospel of Jesus and his Church. This implies a Baptism of desire (CCC 1258-1260).

Children who die without receiving Baptism are entrusted into the merciful arms of the all-loving God, who gives salvation to whomever he chooses (CCC 1257, 1261). "Limbo," a natural place of happiness for infants who die without Baptism, was commonly taught until after Vatican II, although it was not a doctrine of the Church.

The question sometimes arises as to whether non-Christians can be saved. Those who do not know of Christ or the Church but seek to know the truth and wish to do God's will according to their understanding can be saved. Vatican II said, "For since Christ died for all, and since all men are in fact called to one and the same destiny, which is divine, we must hold that the Holy Spirit offers to all the possibility of being made partners, in a way known to God, in the paschal mystery."[7]

Baptism opens us up to God's graces. We become a new creation through it when we are reborn in the Holy Spirit. It cleanses us of all sins, and we are forgiven through the waters of Baptism.

Our new life is sometimes referred to as the state of sanctifying, or habitual, grace. It is a state of blessedness that makes us friends of God and heirs of eternal life. Baptism gives us actual graces to help us grow in virtue, avoid sin, and lead a good life. We also receive special sacramental graces, as well as theological and moral virtues that assist us in developing spiritual habits and in avoiding sinful ones. We become God's adopted sons and daughters, partakers of God's divine nature, and temples of the Holy Spirit.

It's difficult to fathom the richness bestowed on a baptized person. Through prayer and reflection, we recognize our worth before God and see others in a new way. How can we hurt others or refuse to forgive them if all of us are God's children? Baptism calls us to love and forgive one another, in imitation of Christ, and to be persons for others.

Writing to the Church at Ephesus, Paul says that "we are members of one another" (Eph 4:25). Baptism makes us members of Christ's Body, the Church. This membership goes beyond age, race, ethnicity, or state in life. We join God's New Covenant people, for "in the one Spirit we were all baptized into one body — Jews or Greeks, slaves or free — and we were all made to drink of one Spirit" (1 Cor 12:13).

We are baptized into Jesus' one holy priesthood and participate in it. This is called the "common priesthood of all believers." Through incorporation into the Church, we join in her mission and ministry, as we serve one another, reach out to non-believers, and help the poor through acts of mercy and social justice.

Baptism, the foundation for the life of grace, changes our spiritual status. We must receive it before receiving the other sacraments. After Baptism, we are not the same as before, for it brings about a real, hidden, and spiritual change in us.

Baptism forever seals us with an indelible mark, or character, which marks us as members of Christ and his Church. Even if a person denies the faith, the seal remains. Unrepentant mortal sin may prevent a person from entering heaven, but it does not eradicate the seal. This seal enables us to participate in liturgical celebrations and receive other sacraments. This seal calls us to commit ourselves to a virtuous life of service in imitation of Jesus, who showed us the way. The seal anticipates God's eternal blessings for a life well lived.

Baptized persons belong to Jesus and to other Christians, as sons and daughters in Christ. This obliges us to follow Church leaders and actively help them carry out their work, for "Baptism . . . constitutes the sacramental bond of unity existing among all who through it are reborn."[8]

To validly receive other sacraments, we need to be baptized. No one can receive the Eucharist, marriage, or any other sacrament before being baptized. All other sacraments flow from Baptism, as from a font. As the *Rite of Baptism* (n. 103) states:

> Dearly beloved, this child has been reborn in baptism. He (she) is now called a child of God, for so indeed he (she) is. In confirmation he (she) will receive the fullness of God's Spirit. In holy communion he (she) will share the banquet of Christ's sacrifice, calling God his (her) Father in the midst of the Church.

The *Code of Canon Law* (CIC, c. 864) states, "Every person not yet baptized and only such a person is capable of baptism." Both adults and children can be baptized. This has been the long-standing Church tradition from the earliest years. Nonetheless, "Since the beginning of the Church, adult Baptism is the common practice where the proclamation of the Gospel is still new" (CCC 1247).

An adult must express a wish to receive Baptism, be instructed in the faith, and give witness to a Christian life. The person is to be sorry for his or her sins. If in danger of death, an adult must manifest in some way an intention to be baptized, must have a rudimentary knowledge of Catholic belief and practices, and must promise to live as a Catholic and observe the commandments (CIC, c. 865 §2). If in danger of death, infants are to be baptized immediately.

Those seeking Baptism need to be incorporated into the Christian community and made to feel a part of it. The *Rite of Christian Initiation of Adults* enables this to happen normally if the parish community supports the candidate or catechumen during the process of initiation into the Church. To assist this effort, godparents must be strong believers, must be active in the practice of their Catholic faith, and must help the catechumen (non-baptized person) or candidate (person baptized in another faith) grow in faith.

The ordinary ministers of Baptism are bishops, priests, and deacons in the Roman Catholic Church. If the person is in danger of death or in an emergency situation, any person can baptize, even one who is not baptized, providing he or she intends to do what the Church intends in this sacrament and uses water and the Trinitarian formula.

The ordinary place for Baptism is in a church. In emergency situations, Baptisms can take place in hospital rooms, at home, on the battlefield, or anywhere else. The Church celebrates Baptisms during the Eucharistic liturgy, outside of Mass, or at other times.

The celebration of Baptism during Mass reflects the connection between Baptism and the outpouring of divine grace from Jesus (the source of all blessings, really present in the Eucharist), and more fully reflects the birth into a community of faith. Baptism at Mass reminds the participants of its association with the Eucharist and its connection with the Paschal Mystery of Jesus' death, resurrection, and ascension.

In the Roman (or Latin) Catholic Church, Baptism is conferred by a triple immersion into the baptismal water or by a triple pouring of baptismal water on a person's head, while saying, "[Name], I baptize you in the name of the Father, and of the Son, and of the Holy Spirit."

In the Eastern Catholic Churches, the person to be baptized faces the East, and the celebrant says, "The servant of God, [name], is baptized in the name of the Father, and of the Son, and of the Holy Spirit" (cf. CCC 1240). At each invocation, the candidate is immersed into the water.

Baptism and Basic Human Needs

The sacrament of Baptism addresses our basic human need to search for purpose and meaning. To delve more deeply, we ask: "As humans, for what do we search?" Often, we don't stop to ask this question. But whether we ask it or not, the search goes on within us.

God has "wired" us to ask such questions as "Who am I?" and "Where will I go after death?" When we put off such questions or look for answers in false places, they still persist.

What are the core human needs that such questions address? God addresses these questions through the revealed Word. Baptism helps us in our search for answers.

The basic human needs relating to Baptism include a search for deeper meaning, answers to life's purpose, a community to probe basic issues, a more meaningful life than this one, and hope.

We first wonder why we need to search for something more. We look deeper than the senses can comprehend. We may ask, "Why does the sun come up in the morning?" and "Who made the sun?" We search for love but are never fully satisfied. We form close bonds with spouses, parents, or friends, but often they are not enough.

The quest for more and the need for connections deeper than this world can give indicate that if life is to make sense, there must be more to it than this world provides. Christians find this *more* in God, revealed by Jesus. He tells us of the new life that God offers to believers. This life begins at Baptism and lasts forever.

Baptism initiates us into the life of God, which deepens as our faith matures. It leads to limited happiness on earth and eternal happiness in heaven. It provides the graces that sustain us on our way. As we enter through the gate of Baptism, we begin our journey to eternal life.

If there were no Baptism or promise of eternal life, where would our life be now? Injustice, senseless suffering, and prolonged illness make little sense without rewards and punishments in the next life. The new life of Baptism elevates us above our present tribulations. Baptism assures us that we will enter eternal life after death, if we follow God's commandments.

The ultimate source of earthly communities is the Trinity. This heavenly community invites us to join it. Life would be lonely if we had to make our journey to our final destiny without an earthly community to support us. We need one another, as we work out our eternal salvation.

God's grace begins in the family that nourishes our faith and prepares us to live out our baptismal commitment. Baptism makes us members of Christ's Mystical Body, not members of a worldly club or organization. It assures us that we don't ever have to be alone, for we belong to the Communion of Saints, God's chosen friends in heaven, on earth, and in purgatory. Wherever we go or whatever we do, this community will stand by us. Faithful living of our baptismal promises guarantees us the help needed to remain faithful to God's calling.

Authentic Christian living means following Jesus by living rightly, acting justly, and being kind to our neighbor. To live this way, we need to cooperate with God's grace, received at Baptism, which invites us to serve our brothers and sisters, as Jesus did. As we follow his way, we discover the true meaning of life.

We find meaning in all sorts of things. We find it in a good movie, a friend's love, a child's smile, money, a job, a car, a computer, or a home. Some kinds of meaning are functional (something we use), and others are ultimate (love, trust, and compassion). We find meaning in things peripheral to our faith, but we need more. Since worldly things cannot satisfy our deepest yearnings, we look to the spiritual life for hope.

We have a built-in need for hope. In a world often without hope, our baptismal commitment helps us appreciate creation as God's beautiful garden. To see what effect it has on us, we consider disaster victims throughout the world and realize that their hope in God often sustains them during terrible ordeals and death. In many instances involving Christians, their baptismal faith consoles them and roots their hope for a better tomorrow.

Hope sets the foundation for the journey of baptized people. The living water we receive when entering the Christian community make possible our journey. Because Jesus died and was raised up, we, too, will rise with him.

ç∞

Communal and Personal Implications

What implications can we draw from this chapter on Baptism for Christian living in our family, neighborhood, work, and church?

As a child, I knew that I was a Catholic with loving parents and siblings, living in St. William's Parish. I never questioned that I belonged in my family or parish. My neighbors and classmates felt the same way. Life was stable and well established.

The yearning for identity went beyond my parents, my home, and my church. It took root in God and showed itself in the need to be connected with him through a like-minded community of parish believers. This brought a feeling of acceptance and welcome. Baptism initiated me into this spiritual community.

Coming to faith involves a journey passing through many gateways. The Christian community nourishes the beginning of faith and its development. The welcome and acceptance that I experienced at my parish as a child was the foundation for my growth in faith:

- The *Rite of Baptism for Children* says, "[Y]ou have become a new creation, and have clothed yourself in Christ . . ." (n. 99). What are the consequences for our moral life of believing that at Baptism we are clothed in Christ?
- What are some implications of seeing Baptism as a gateway?
- Reflect on the effects in your life, when you realize that Baptism seals you with an indelible spiritual mark that forever identifies you as joined to Christ.
- If you have a difficult time with a person at home or at work, consider him or her as a child of God and see if this helps you get along with the person.
- Consider what your baptismal commitment should mean for your life at home and at work. What new insights have you derived from this chapter? What are their implications for your life?
- The *Catechism of the Catholic Church* says, "Baptism is necessary for salvation for those to whom the Gospel has been proclaimed and who have had the possibility of asking for this sacrament." (CCC 1257). How does this apply to non-Christian friends and family? How can they be saved?
- The *Rite of Christian Initiation of Adults* welcomes and incorporates those seeking

Baptism into the Christian community and makes them feel a part of it. What may happen if they do not feel a part of a community?

- Although the Church encourages parents to have a child baptized within weeks of its birth, why do you think there is a growing practice of putting off a child's baptism for months after birth?
- How does a parish's sense of welcome and hospitality influence people, as they consider having a child baptized?
- If members of your family or your friends have not had their children baptized, what can you do to encourage them to do so?

෩

CHAPTER THREE

୶

Confirmation

Gateway to Deeper Union With the Holy Spirit and the Church

IN THE SPRING OF 1942, I was eight years old and in the second grade at St. William's School. Earlier in the school year, we made our first confession and received our First Communion.

I had ambiguous feelings when preparing for Confirmation. Weeks before I received this sacrament, Sister Matilda, our teacher, told us that Confirmation makes us strong and faithful soldiers of Jesus Christ. She said it is a sacrament of Christian maturity and gives us the grace to defend our faith. This sounded strange, for we were little kids, and I wondered how we could be mature soldiers at our age.

She went on to explain that in order to indicate that we were mature Christians, ready to die for our faith, during the Confirmation ceremony the bishop would slap us gently on the cheek to remind us of our role as mature Christians. To scare us, upper-grade students told us that we would get a really hard slap that would hurt. The whole thing seemed strange to me. I wanted to live, not die.

On the evening of my confirmation, this confused second-grader entered the church. About the only thing that I remember is the bishop coming into church, putting the oil on my head, and giving me a gentle slap on the cheek. The sister was right; it was a gentle slap, not the kind the older kids had teased us about.

This description of the *Rite of Confirmation* sounds strange today because after Vatican II, the sacrament took on a different flavor. There was no more slap or focus on becoming a mature Christian, ready to give up one's life for the faith. Instead, as the second of the three sacraments of Christian initiation, Confirmation is received to strengthen our initial faith and help us grow in the Catholic faith.

The *Rite of Christian Initiation of Adults* offers new norms for the three sacraments of initiation. During this rite, the celebrant confirms adults and some children at the Easter Vigil. At other times, the bishop (or priests delegated by him) confirms children in the seventh or eighth grade and others in high school.

The Eastern Catholic Churches refer to this sacrament as "Chrismation." A bishop or priest confirms children immediately after Baptism and prior to receiving a drop of consecrated wine, the blood of Jesus, in their First Communion.

What are the reasons for such variety? What is the history and theology behind the sacrament of

Confirmation? And most important for our consideration, to what is Confirmation a gateway?

Confirmation as a Gateway

Confirmation is a partner to Baptism. Both were part of the same ritual celebration in the early Church. After immersion into baptismal water, the candidate was taken out, dried off, and "confirmed" or blessed by the bishop as a new Christian (neophyte). The person then went into church to receive the Eucharist. This continuous action of Baptism, Confirmation, and the Eucharist, celebrating Christian initiation, introduced him or her into the kingdom of God and the Church.

In *Understanding the Sacraments Today*, Lawrence Mick writes:

> Everything that Baptism means and everything to which it commits us is what confirmation reaffirms. As a sacrament of initiation, confirmation is a beginning, not an ending. Too often seen as the end of a student's religious education, it should rather be the beginning of a deeper level of Christian living. As a reaffirmation of Baptism, it can be a time to undertake the Christian way of life with new vigor and deeper commitment.[9]

To answer why the neophyte is confirmed and what it symbolizes, we must consider Christian initiation. Baptism is the beginning of a lifelong process whereby we continue to grow into the love of God and service of our neighbor. This growth in faith is part of the *conversion process*.

Confirmation is about *conversion*, regardless of what age it is received. To prepare for it, the Church community often gives catechumens and candidates a Bible, catechizes them in the Scriptures and Church teaching, and prays for them. These preparations set the stage for those persons receiving the grace of the Holy Spirit. They also enhance the candidates' conversion process, thus leading to growth in faith. They help the persons become more deeply united with Christ and the community of believers.

Confirmation opens us to continued growth in Christ, and its ongoing graces help us on the path toward Christian adulthood. The sacrament of Confirmation completes the baptismal grace. The recipient receives special strength and help, given by the Holy Spirit, and is more perfectly united to the Body of Christ, the Church (CCC 1285).

The grace bestowed in Confirmation lasts our entire lives. Just as Christian conversion is a living, flowing reality, so also are the graces of Confirmation that lead us more deeply into the Paschal Mystery. When having doubts about faith, wondering why a loved one suffers, or debating whether to change jobs, the graces of Confirmation are spiritual helps inviting us to discern God's will. With their help, we can respond to Jesus' call every day to follow him, as we walk the road to eternal life.

History of Confirmation

The Old Testament hints at the Holy Spirit's role in our liberation from the sin of Adam. Isaiah prophesied that the Spirit of God would rest on the future Messiah (Is 11:2, 61:1). Mary fulfilled this prophecy when she conceived Jesus by the power of the Holy Spirit. It was further revealed when the Holy Spirit came upon Jesus at his baptism by John in the Jordan River. Jesus promised to send the Holy Spirit to remain with the Church. He fulfilled this promise at Pentecost. The Holy Spirit inspired Jesus' disciples to go into the world and proclaim Jesus as Lord.

Paul's Letter to the Hebrews describes the laying on of hands as a key aspect of Christian growth. The *Catechism of the Catholic Church* says:

> Very early, the better to signify the gift of the Holy Spirit, an anointing with perfumed oil (*chrism*) was added to the laying on of hands. This anointing highlights the name "Christian," which means "anointed" and derives from that of Christ himself whom God "anointed with the Holy Spirit" (Acts 10:38). (CCC 1289; emphasis in original)

This unity of immersion into water, anointing, and imposition of hands gradually shifted focus as the Church grew in numbers. As mentioned in the chapter on Baptism, infant and child baptism existed in the early Church. However, with the cessation of persecutions of Christians after 313 (Edict of Milan), the rapid spread of the faith throughout the Roman Empire, and the increased number of households brought about a gradual shift from mostly adult baptismal candidates to a greater number of children's baptisms.

With the rise in infant baptisms and the movement of Christians to rural areas, it was not as easy for bishops to administer the sacraments. A separate sacrament of Confirmation emerged, referred to by Tertullian and also by Hippolytus in the latter's *Apostolic Traditions*.

Confirmation took on a different focus in the Latin (Western) and Eastern Catholic Churches. The Latin Catholic Church emphasized the unity of the baptized person with the bishop by reserving the administration of Confirmation to the bishop. This unity with the bishop stressed the unity of the entire Church and its origin with the apostles. The *Catechism of the Catholic Church* says:

> In the West the desire to reserve the completion of Baptism to the bishop caused the temporary separation of the two sacraments [Baptism and Confirmation]. . . . A

custom of the Roman Church facilitated
the development of the Western practice:
a double anointing with sacred chrism after Baptism. The first anointing of the neophyte on coming out of the baptismal bath
was performed by the priest; it was completed by a second anointing on the forehead of the newly baptized by the bishop.
(CCC 1290-1291)

This first anointing with chrism is still part of
the baptismal rite. The second is reserved to Confirmation.

Eastern Catholic Churches approach this challenge differently. Chrismation complements Baptism
as an aspect of the process of initiation. It is a sacrament of the Holy Spirit, a powerful sign that marks
the person as belonging to Christ.

The Eastern churches stressed the unity of
Christian initiation, thus maintaining the unity of
the order of Baptism, Confirmation, and the Eucharist, even though the bishop was no longer the
celebrant at all Confirmations. The sacrament was
often administered by the priest after Baptism. The
bishop, however, continued to consecrate the myron (holy oil used in the ceremony). In so doing, he
maintained an episcopal connection with all baptisms and confirmations.

During the second millennium, Confirmation
was associated in the Latin Church with becoming a

mature Christian, thus losing its primary focus with Baptism as part of an ongoing initiation into the dying and rising of Jesus at various life stages.

The Council of Trent maintained the separation of the Rites of Initiation. Consequently, many persons received Confirmation later in life or not at all. The council insisted, however, that it is a sacrament, in direct opposition to the Protestants who denied this teaching.

The liturgical reforms of Vatican II changed the direction of Confirmation. Rather than focus on maturity, Confirmation now centers on a person's ongoing initiation into Christ, the Christian life, and the Church. The council took no definitive stand on the order of the sacraments of initiation after Baptism, but some liturgists prefer returning to the original ordering of Baptism, Confirmation, and the Eucharist. The local bishop makes the final decision on this matter and decides the appropriate age when the candidate receives the sacrament of Confirmation.

Basic Church Teachings on Confirmation

Like Baptism, the Holy Spirit is closely associated with Confirmation, and like all of God's creation, the graces produced by Confirmation are the work of the entire Trinity. Just as the Holy Spirit descended on

Jesus at his baptism and on the assembled disciples on Pentecost, so also the Holy Spirit enlivens the souls of the baptized and confirmed.

Confirmation roots us more deeply with the Father, joins us more fully with Jesus and the Church, and increases within us the gifts of the Holy Spirit. It makes these gifts more complete and enables us to witness to Christ in spreading the faith and defending it against attacks and errors. The Sign of the Cross used during the rites of initiation strengthens us, as we celebrate the cross as a sign of victory over sin and death.

Baptized persons receive a permanent seal, or mark; so do those receiving Confirmation. Even if people deny their faith and later profess it again, these sacraments are not repeated, for their seals and permanent effects remain.

Baptism initiates us into the common priesthood. The graces flowing from Confirmation perfect this priesthood of the faithful and give us the "power to profess faith in Christ publicly" (CCC 1305) and the graces necessary to discern God's calling regardless of the circumstances.

The *Catechism of the Catholic Church* says:

> *In the Latin Rite*, the ordinary minister of Confirmation is the bishop. If the need arises, the bishop may grant the faculty of administering Confirmation to priests, although it is

fitting that he confer it himself, mindful that the celebration of Confirmation has been temporarily separated from Baptism for this reason. (CCC 1313; emphasis in original)

In danger of death, any priest can administer Confirmation.

The Eastern Catholic Churches also regard Chrismation as a sacrament. The bishop uses the words "The seal of the gift of the Holy Spirit" as he imposes hands and anoints the person with myron, or chrism. Baptism and Chrismation represent two dimensions of the mystery of initiation into the dying and rising with Jesus (Baptism) and our reception of the gifts of the Holy Spirit (Chrismation). Baptism — Chrismation — leads us into the mystery of Trinitarian life and into the Mystical Body of Christ.

Every baptized person can and should receive the sacrament of Confirmation. Without it, full Christian initiation (that is, Baptism, Confirmation, and the Eucharist) is incomplete. This sacrament focuses on conversion, not on the best age to receive it. In this regard, *Understanding the Sacraments Today* says:

So with confirmation, the process of conversion precedes and follows the ritual celebration. The actual timing of the ritual moment is not nearly as important as the process it celebrates. . . . Whether confirmation is celebrated around an eight-day-old or an eighty-year-old person, the Church must make sure that there is a process of conversion linked to it and flowing from it. Without such conversion, the sacrament will become an empty ritual at any age.[10]

Confirmation is not necessary for salvation; neither is it required for a valid Christian marriage. Nonetheless, if possible, it should be received before the marriage celebration. As the *Code of Canon Law* states, "Catholics who have not yet received the sacrament of confirmation are to receive it before they are admitted to marriage if it can be done without grave inconvenience" (CIC, c. 1065 §1).

Confirmation is required before a candidate for the religious life enters the novitiate. (CIC, c. 645 §1). To be promoted to sacred orders, a candidate must show documentation that he has been confirmed (CIC, c. 1050, 3°). It is also necessary for a person to be a sponsor at a Catholic Baptism (CIC, c. 874 §1, 3°).

Because of shifting emphasis in the Latin Church over the centuries, some refer to Confirmation as a sacrament without a theology. This indicates Confirmation's flexibility, allowing it to adapt as circumstances demand. Although Confirmation has a somewhat ambiguous history, it is an important sacrament, bestowing God's grace on our ongoing journey to eternity. At every juncture, it is a gateway leading to a richer and more blessed life.

Confirmation and Basic Human Needs

One of the ways that Confirmation is a gateway is that it helps us address basic human needs, especially the need for completeness, permanency, and ongoing growth as we move through the stages and challenges of our lives.

Regardless of age, we strive for completeness. As long as we live, our work is not finished. The need to grow is inherent in every person: either we grow or we die. The same applies to the spiritual life. Jesus indicated the need for constant growth. He compared the kingdom of God to a mustard seed that grows into a mature tree. The growth of God's kingdom, like the mustard seed, starts small and grows to spiritual maturity with the help of God's grace.

Since Confirmation produces an indelible mark, its permanent nature bestows special graces on the recipient when challenges arise. These graces move us in new directions and invite us into deeper levels of spiritual conversion. When we cooperate with the graces of Confirmation, we live in union with God and celebrate the Eucharist as faithful members of Christ's Body.

We grow and adapt according to the times and situations where we find ourselves. Sometimes, this means refocusing our priorities and modes of action.

Take the student athlete who had his sights set on a professional football career. He was good enough, and in his senior college year he anticipated being chosen in the professional draft.

Then, in his next-to-last game, he blew out his knee, which ended his football career. Imagine his trauma and mental pain when realizing that all the years of preparation now meant nothing! He had to readjust and change directions.

This same adjustment applies to a woman losing her job or to a man whose heart attack, when he is forty years old, prohibits him from continuing in construction work.

The sacrament of Confirmation gives us special graces to meet such difficulties with faith and courage, and it provides the hope we need to sustain us in hard times, as we unite our pain with Jesus' suffering and death.

If we look for a virtue to typify Confirmation, we might consider *wisdom*. Wisdom comes from God. In the Old Testament, "Wisdom" often referred to God himself. The Jews considered it among the greatest virtues. The graces of Confirmation move us toward maturity in the faith. What better gift can we ask for to achieve maturity than the gift of wisdom? Our openness to cooperate with this gift brings Christian maturity.

Whenever we come to a fork in life's road and move forward on a new and unclear path, Confirmation unleashes the floodgates of God's graces to help us gain wisdom and change direction.

❧

COMMUNAL AND PERSONAL IMPLICATIONS

What implications can we draw from this chapter on Confirmation for Christian living in our family, neighborhood, work, and church?

Once, I asked students in a sacramental theology class at a Catholic university which sacrament was very important to them. Their responses surprised me. I expected to hear "Baptism" or "the Eucharist." Instead, many described their Confirmation. When I asked why it was very important, they said it was the only sacrament where they initially had a choice. Most parents and pastors allowed them to decide whether they were ready to receive it. Some were confirmed, others put it off until later, and still others never received this sacrament. Those given a choice became aware of a budding wisdom within them. Most accepted their Christian responsibilities more seriously than if the matter had been decided for them.

Take a few moments to reflect on the above comments on Confirmation or on those listed below:

- How is Confirmation a gateway, and how does it strengthen us in the Catholic faith? How can we teach this to our loved ones about to be confirmed?

- Looking back to your Confirmation, how can you see that the gift of wisdom, given at Confirmation, was valuable when making important family decisions or those affecting your future? How can we foster this gift?
- Reflect on the following statement: Just as Christian conversion is a living, flowing reality, so also are the graces of Confirmation that lead us more deeply into the Paschal Mystery. How does this apply to your life?
- Confirmation increases the graces of the Holy Spirit within us and enables us to witness to Christ, to spread the faith, and to defend it against attacks and errors. How does this apply to your life of prayer and speak of the importance of frequent reception of the sacraments?
- How can we help the broader community of the faithful to recognize the value of Confirmation in increasing the gifts of the Holy Spirit within us, thus enabling us to witness to Christ and defend our faith against prejudice? How can we witness to Christ in our family, at work, and among friends?

- What value is there in reflecting on the gifts of the Holy Spirit, received in Confirmation, when life becomes tedious?
- Meditate on how we can recognize for ourselves, and help others see, that co-operation with the graces of the Holy Spirit received at Confirmation helps us live in closer union with God, celebrate the Eucharist more deeply, and be happier persons.
- How would you explain the meaning and importance of Confirmation to people preparing to receive this sacrament?
- Why should every baptized person receive the sacrament of Confirmation? Consider the implications of not receiving it.
- Why do you think that children should or should not receive Confirmation at the same time as Baptism?
- What do you think is the best age to receive Confirmation? Why?

౮

CHAPTER FOUR

∽

Eucharist

*Gateway Celebrating God's Eternal Love
and the Eternal Mystery of Jesus' Passion,
Death, Resurrection, and Ascension*

THE SUN FAILED TO SHINE on the day that I celebrated Mass at home with my mother, the Sunday after Dad died. Mom and I were grieving, and the gloom outside reflected the hollowness in our hearts.

When we gathered for Mass at the dining room table, a profound awe overtook us during the prayers and readings. The post-Resurrection stories spoke of life beyond the grave.

That day, the Eucharist had special depth and power. After Communion, we sat in silence for a long time. I thought of Jesus' time with his friends at the Last Supper. His agony and death touched my heart. As memories flooded my soul, I felt Jesus' intimate presence within me. In the simplicity of our home, the Eucharist led Mom and me toward a fuller life here and eternal life hereafter.

I never experienced the Eucharist more intently as a gateway to eternity than I did that Sunday morning at our dining room table.

The Eucharist invites us into God's eternal love and into the mystery of Jesus' Passion, death, resurrection, and ascension. Vatican II describes it as "the source and summit of the Christian life."[11] All other sacraments, Church ministries, prayers, and works of social justice flow from the Eucharist and lead back to it, for the Eucharist is Jesus, the savior of the world.

Jesus confirms that the Eucharist is the principle gateway through which we pass to reach eternal life, when he says: "Very truly, I tell you, unless you eat the flesh of the Son of Man and drink his blood, you have no life in you. Those who eat my flesh and drink my blood have eternal life, and I will raise them up on the last day" (Jn 6:53-54).

In fifty years as a priest, I have celebrated the Eucharist in parish churches, cathedrals, religious communities, schools, universities, nursing homes, and state parks (sometimes with thousands in attendance; at other times, alone). During these celebrations, the language, style, and arrangement changed, but the core of the Eucharist remained the same.

Every time I preside at Mass, I call upon Jesus in words and actions, for he is the principle priest of the Mass. As the assembled community remembers his Paschal Mystery, Jesus comes on the altar, offering us the blessings that he gained through his sacrificial death on the cross, offering us a gateway to eternal life.

The Eucharist as a Gateway

I walked along a small stream flowing gently over rocks, mud, and twigs. In one place, it curved into an almost perfect circle, leaving an island in the water. Over the past five years, I watched as the water gradually made its way along a tree root and broke through the small parcel of land that kept the stream from flowing smoothly in a straight line that avoided the "U" bypass.

In the mud caused by the stream flooding, raccoon and bird tracks reminded me of their presence earlier that day. As the stream continued to flow, it passed over large rocks. Its gently babbling sounds became louder as it prepared to go through a narrow, deep gorge. When the water sped up, the gorge became the gateway through which the stream passed to enter a larger stream that eventually joined the main channel of the river.

As I stood by the gorge, watching the small stream get faster and stronger, I remembered the Eucharist. Like the gorge, the Eucharist is the gateway for all life-giving streams of grace to flow from the cross into the Body of Christ, the Church. This grace springs from Jesus' death and resurrection.

The Eucharist makes present Jesus' Paschal Mystery. Just as streams that feed a river pass through gorges, over rocks, and into smooth places, so do the sacraments, prayers, and good actions flow from the Eucharist as their source. Because of it, we glorify

God, "as it was in the beginning, is now, and ever shall be, world without end. Amen."

History of the Eucharist

The Eucharist is the third sacrament of initiation. Its early history shows its connection with Baptism and Confirmation in the ancient rites of Christian initiation. This history helps us appreciate the Eucharist as a gateway to the Christian life and to the other sacraments.

The Jews of the Old Covenant offered bread and wine as the first fruits of their work to thank God and express their gratitude. Exodus recounts the story of the Jewish liberation from slavery in Egypt, repeated each year at Passover, when unleavened bread took on special significance as a perpetual reminder of God's liberation of the Jews. The cup of blessing at Passover reminded them of the messianic expectation. Manna, a gift of God, sustained the Jews in the desert. These symbols took on new meaning when Jesus inaugurated his New Covenant and instituted the Eucharist at the Last Supper.

The Eucharist originates with Jesus' celebration of his final meal on earth with his disciples, before he suffered and died. In this meal, he joins the Jewish Passover meal with his upcoming death. He is the Paschal victim ushering in the New Covenant in a sacrifice not made with the blood of calves or bulls but with his own blood.

The New Testament contains four versions of Jesus' institution of the Eucharist at the Last Supper. These come from two distinct traditions describing the Last Supper: the Pauline-Lukan tradition (Lk 22:19-20 parallels 1 Cor 11:23-26) and the Markan tradition (Mk 14:24 parallels Mt 26:27-28). These may have been liturgical formulas used in early Christianity. The sixth chapter of John, where Jesus refers to himself as "the bread of life," may also be an early liturgical text.

The Liturgy of the Eucharist focuses on the Eucharistic meal as a perpetual remembrance of Jesus' Paschal Mystery. The words pronounced over the bread and wine remind us of the historical roots of the Eucharist in the Last Supper and the cross. Melchizedek's offering of bread and wine prefigured Jesus' offering at the Last Supper (Gen 14:18-20).

Concerning the Eucharist, the *Catechism of the Catholic Church* says:

> Jesus' passing over to his father by his death and Resurrection, the new Passover, is anticipated in the [Last] Supper and celebrated in the Eucharist, which fulfills the Jewish Passover and anticipates the final Passover of the Church in the glory of the kingdom. (CCC 1340)

At the Last Supper, Jesus commanded his disciples to "do this in memory of me." Early Christians, after Pentecost, followed his instructions and gathered regularly to celebrate the "Lord's Table." The Acts of the Apostles states:

> They devoted themselves to the apostles' teaching and fellowship, to the breaking of bread and the prayers. . . . Day by day, as they spent much time together in the temple, they broke bread at home and ate their food with glad and generous hearts. (Acts 2:42, 46)

As the Church began, Christians gathered on Sunday, the first day of the week, to break bread, remembering that Jesus rose from the dead on this day. For a while, this gathering included a communal, agape meal with food and drink, followed by the breaking of the bread (the Eucharist). Eventually, after the agape meal was dropped, the rite that remained was short. To it was added "a service of the Word, which was modeled on the Sabbath liturgy of the synagogue."[12]

At this ritual, the assembled faithful read from the Old and New Testaments and from readings and memories of the apostles and martyrs. They prayed and sang, and the celebrant urged them to live by the teachings that they heard. They prayed for themselves and others, gave thanks, exchanged a kiss, and offered gifts of bread and wine. The faithful received the Eucharistic gifts, and after the service they took the Eucharist to the sick and dying.

Persecution of the early Church brought danger to those who assembled for instruction and for the breaking of the bread. Consequently, preparation for entrance into the body of the faithful became a long and careful process. Initiation rites usually lasted several years, with the catechumens (those under instruction) dismissed before the community celebrated the Eucharist. These rites climaxed with candidates being admitted into full communion with the Church through the reception of Baptism, Confirmation, and the Eucharist.

Constantine's conversion in the year 312 had enormous ramifications for Eucharistic liturgies. He granted freedom of religion to all those in the empire. Many became Christians, including royal officials. This brought the splendor of the old Roman assemblies and public officials into the liturgy, and some of the pomp associated with them entered into liturgical celebrations.

During this time, a transition occurred from celebrating the Eucharist in Greek to the vernacular language, which, at the time, was Latin. Pope St. Damasus I (304-384), who commissioned St. Jerome (c. 340-420) to prepare a Latin translation of the Scriptures (known as the "Vulgate"), is often credited with introducing Latin into the liturgy.

After the Edict of Milan (313) granted freedom of religion, significant changes occurred. In the eighth century, Pippin and his son Charlemagne desired closer ties to Rome, so they adapted the Roman liturgy for the Frankish kingdom. This adaptation included a dynamic and creative spirit. They also added a Palm Sunday liturgy and Easter Vigil rites. In time, this liturgy made its way back to Rome, and during his pontificate (1073-1085) Pope St. Gregory VII decreed its use for the entire Latin Catholic Church.

A gradual liturgical dissolution occurred during the next centuries. The Mass became the priest's business, a sense of community disappeared, the Communion rail was added, the Latin language became an obstacle to the attendees, and few people received Communion. Participants focused on looking at the host, instead of receiving it at Mass. The high point of the Mass happened at the Consecration, when the priest elevated the host. At the Consecration, some even yelled out, "Raise it higher, Friar!" This ocular Communion (looking at the consecrated host but not physically receiving it) set the stage for popular devotions like the feast of Corpus Christi.

From the thirteenth century onward, movement away from receiving the Eucharist as spiritual food and toward viewing the consecrated host, especially after Mass, led to rituals that honored Jesus' presence in the consecrated Eucharistic bread outside of Mass. These included Perpetual Adoration and Forty Hours Devotion. In the latter devotion, a consecrated host is exposed on the altar in a gold vessel, called a "monstrance," over a period of forty hours.

The Latin Catholic liturgy was in need of reform during the Late Middle Ages. Abuses crept in, which included a lack of appreciation of the Eucharistic food, a focus on the Mass as belonging to the priest, and the selling of Mass stipends. The Protestant Reformation, influenced by changes initiated by Luther and Calvin, stressed communal participation in the liturgy and denounced abuses surrounding Mass stipends that came from overdemanding clerics. These Protestant reformers adopted theological positions incompatible with the Church's belief in the Real Presence and the Sacrifice of the Mass. The Council of Trent condemned their positions, clarified basic teachings on the Eucharist, and set the parameters for Catholic worship before Vatican II.

In 1963, the Second Vatican Council issued the Constitution on the Sacred Liturgy (*Sacrosanctum Concilium*). It introduced the vernacular language, stressed the community's role, decreed the reform of the *Roman Missal*, reintroduced a rite of initiation for receiving catechumens into the Church, and reestablished the Easter Vigil.

These changes had a widespread effect as liturgical celebrations became community events and as the laity recognized their role as the People of God. Lay ministers grew in numbers, lay women and men ministered as altar attendants and lectors, the diaconate was reintroduced, and the vernacular languages replaced Latin. A new edition of the *Roman Missal* followed, along with revisions of the liturgical texts associated with the other sacraments.

Basic Church Teachings on the Eucharist

As stated earlier, at the Last Supper Jesus commanded his disciples to "do this . . . in remembrance of
me" (1 Cor 11:25). This happens at every Mass, which
is a memorial of his sacrifice on the cross.

When participating in the Eucharist, we return
to the Father, through our offering, the gifts and
blessings we have received from him. These include
all of creation and the simple gifts of bread and wine,
which through a miraculous transformation become
the body and blood of Jesus. This happens by the
power of the Holy Spirit and the words of Christ,
spoken by the priest. Through the priest's actions,
Christ becomes really present on the altar — body
and blood, soul and divinity (CCC 1357).

The Eucharist is an act of thanksgiving and praise
as well as a sacrificial memorial, offered by Jesus to
his Father, which we share as members of his Mystical Body. Jesus offers to the Father his eternal sacrifice
on the cross that brought about our redemption. This
sacrificial memorial gives us hope in a world often
without hope, for Christ is really present "by the power of his word and of his *Spirit*" (CCC 1358; emphasis
in original). Only a bishop or priest may preside at the
Eucharistic celebration. Deacons may assist.

The word "Eucharist" comes from a Greek word
meaning "thanksgiving." After the Resurrection,

Jesus' disciples remembered that he gave them the bread and cup at the Last Supper and told them to do the same in memory of him. Their hearts filled with gratitude as they celebrated the breaking of the bread as an act of thanksgiving.

In the breaking of the bread, the disciples thanked Jesus for his suffering on the cross and praised him, for "[i]n the Eucharistic sacrifice the whole of creation loved by God is presented to the Father through the death and the Resurrection of Christ" (CCC 1359).

In the Eucharist, we thank God for creating the universe, for sanctifying us, and for redeeming us from Adam's sin and our personal sins. We praise God in the name of all creation, while remembering the great hymns of praise in the Hebrew psalms. At the end of the Eucharistic Prayer, we make our prayer to the Father in union with Jesus and the Holy Spirit: "Through him, and with him, and in him, O God, almighty Father, in the unity of the Holy Spirit. . . ." Appreciating the Mass as an act of praise and thanksgiving makes it easier for us to see that at Mass we honor and worship God as well as pray for ourselves.

The anamnesis — the prayer of remembering, immediately following the Consecration — of the Second Eucharistic Prayer begins, "Therefore, as we celebrate the memorial of his Death and Resurrection. . . ." After Jesus — through the words of the priest — changes bread and wine into his own body and blood, we remember what God does for us. Remembering was very important for Jews in the Old Testament. Steeped in this tradition, it became an essential part of the Christian liturgy.

Remembering is important in our lives. We develop family genealogies to remember our ancestors. Their stories are our stories. In like manner, we pause at the heart of the Eucharistic liturgy to remember what Jesus did for us, as he instructed us to do at the Last Supper. We remember what he did to win eternal life for us through his Paschal Mystery.

The Mass is the memorial of his passing from death to life, where Jesus makes present again his sacrificial offering on the cross and his resurrection. As the *Catechism of the Catholic Church* says:

> [T]he sacrifice Christ offered once for all on the cross remains ever present. "As often as the sacrifice of the Cross by which 'Christ our Pasch has been sacrificed' is celebrated on the altar, the work of redemption is carried out." (CCC 1364)

Because the Eucharist re-presents the sacrifice of the cross, it is a sacrifice. Because it applies the fruits of Christ's crucifixion to humankind, it is a memorial. On the altar and on Calvary, the victim and principle priest are the same — namely, Jesus Christ. The sacrifice of Christ on the cross and the sacrifice of the Mass are one and the same sacrifice.

Since the Church is the Body of Christ, the Mass is also her sacrifice. The entire Church unites with Christ in his offering to the Father. United with Jesus the head, she offers herself to the Father. In so doing, she unites herself with Catholics all over the world, and with the souls in heaven and in purgatory, to give infinite praise and thanks to God.

Jesus' presence in the Eucharist is unique. The Council of Trent taught that "the whole Christ is truly, really, and substantially contained" in the Eucharist.[13] When Trent used the word "really," it meant that Christ is present in the fullest sense. The very substance of Christ, true God and true man, is wholly and completely present.

The Eucharist is not a mere representation or memory of Christ; it is really him, body and blood, soul and divinity. The words of Christ spoken by the priest and the power of the Holy Spirit cause this wondrous change, unexplainable by human reason.

The Latin Church calls this transformation "transubstantiation" (literally meaning "change of substance"). At the Consecration of the Mass, the whole substance of bread and wine is changed into the whole substance of the body and blood of Christ, while the external appearances of bread and wine remain the same. Since the substances actually change, the word "transubstantiation" is used.

Before the Consecration, bread and wine have the "substance" and "accidents" of bread. Afterward, the consecrated species retain the appearance (the accidents) of bread and wine, but the substance is changed into that of the Risen Christ. To help clarify this terminology, "substance" refers to a being that can exist in itself — like a human being or a dog. An "accident" — such as the color green or red, or the taste of something like bread or wine — cannot exist unless some substance sustains it.

A discussion of Christ's Eucharistic presence is incomplete without mentioning the four modes of Christ's presence at Mass. He is present in the body of the faithful, gathered to celebrate the Eucharistic sacrifice. He is present in the Word proclaimed. He is present in the person of the priest who presides at the Eucharist. And he is uniquely present in the Eucharistic species of bread and wine, offered to the Father and received by the faithful.[14]

The Eucharist is a sacrament of forgiveness. Early in the Mass, we ask God to forgive our sins so that we might approach the Eucharist with a clean heart. Through the Mass, we ask for God's forgiveness. The Eucharist forgives venial sins. As the *Catechism of the Catholic Church* says, "[T]he Eucharist strengthens our charity . . . and this living charity *wipes away venial sins*" (CCC 1394; emphasis in original).[15] In the case of mortal sins not previously confessed, we have to confess them in the sacrament of Reconciliation before receiving Holy Communion.

The Latin Church uses unleavened bread. Consecrated bread, not distributed in Holy Communion, is kept in a special container known as the "tabernacle."

Ordinarily, it is located somewhere around the altar, often in the back of the sanctuary. Some churches have a special place of reservation in a side chapel. The Eastern Catholic Churches use leavened bread. Both Latin and Eastern churches use grape wine.

Consecrated Eucharistic bread, given to the dying, is called "Holy Viaticum" (literally meaning "on the way with you"). It is the last sacrament that a person receives *on the way* home to God. This practice continues the long tradition that began in early Church history, where consecrated bread was reserved and kept in a special place, to be given to the sick and dying.

The Eucharist and Basic Human Needs

Our basic needs go beyond the time and place where we live. They include the need for roots, identity, meaning, nourishment, and connection to something beyond us. The Eucharist provides these in the most perfect way we can experience on earth. They root us to our God, the goal of our striving.

We need connections. With parents, children, and grandparents often living in other cities, or having jobs that take them far away, we need a foundation to root our lives. We develop friendships, only to have our friends move away, or we ourselves move away because of work commitments, new jobs, or military service.

What gives us a sense of stability and community? A young woman sitting near me asked this question on a plane trip from Cincinnati to Los Angeles, after seeing me correct theology papers. She wondered about my religion and job. When I told her that I was a priest, she introduced herself as Marci and said she once was Catholic. Not feeling spiritually fed in her parish, Marci joined a Bible-based community church. Then she showed me her Bible, saying, "This and my community give me answers to my questions and root my life." Marci was a searching person who didn't learn much about the Bible and the Eucharist, nor did she develop a sense of Christian community in her former parish. It's sad to hear such stories, especially knowing how the Mass and the Eucharist can center our lives and connect us with a vibrant faith community that appreciates its meaning.

Would Marci have left, if she believed that the Eucharist is really Jesus, the Son of God, who enters her body and sanctifies it, when she receives Communion?

We need to be well informed about the Eucharist because it is the foundation for the path we follow to do good and avoid evil. It is the foundation of our Catholic identity. We often search for identity in a materialistic culture that cannot answer our deepest questions. We need faith in God, for we are created to live in union with God. Catholic identity rests in union with Jesus, the source and summit of our striving. Here, we find our true identity, which we celebrate in the Eucharist.

Our search for identity centers on finding our purpose in life and place in the universe. We cannot discover this without knowing why God made us. As a child, I learned from the *Baltimore Catechism* that God made me to know, love, and serve God, and to be happy with him forever in heaven. To make this possible, God sent Jesus to bring us salvation. On our path, we encounter obstacles. Being faithful requires constant support from God and the Christian community.

As a sacrament of initiation, the Eucharist provides this support. Conversion is a continual process, and the Eucharist anchors our initiation into the mystery of Jesus' death and resurrection. His Paschal Mystery gives us clues as to why we are here. We need the Eucharist to assure us that the graces of Baptism continue through Jesus' sacrifice, made present at each Mass.

The body and blood of Christ in the Eucharist is our best nourishment. Just as Jesus once fed five thousand in the desert, now he gives us the Eucharist, the bread that comes down from heaven.

Christ's resurrected body, received in the Eucharist, bursts asunder earthly ties and opens up the new life won by Jesus on the cross. He lives among us and invites us to love him and serve others. Easter jolted Jesus' followers into a new awareness that life is more than meets the eye. It also inspires us to renew the mystery of our salvation every time we celebrate Mass.

↜

COMMUNAL AND PERSONAL IMPLICATIONS

What implications can we draw from this chapter on the Eucharist for a better understanding of the Eucharist as a gateway and for more fruitful participation in the sacrament?

Today, many Catholics do not understand the meaning of the Mass. Some view it negatively as one more thing to do on Sunday. Others cease attending Mass or go when convenient.

We need to continually grow in appreciation of the Mass and help others to do so. For parents, this means setting a good example for their children by attending Mass with them and seeing that they are well instructed. For all, it means spending time meditating on Christ's real presence.

We can prepare for Sunday Mass by looking at the Sunday readings ahead of time. To enhance our appreciation of the Eucharist, we can listen carefully as the Word is proclaimed at Mass, be attentive to the homily, and draw implications for our life. We can continue our reflections on the meaning of the readings afterward. To do so, we can get a book containing these readings and reflect on them alone, with friends, or with family members.

We may also attend lectures, read pamphlets, and look at programs on the Internet.

To help us make the Mass a key focus of our life, take a few moments to reflect on the following ideas:

- Spend time alone or with others reflecting on the Eucharist as really Christ Jesus, who made us, loves us in spite of our sins, and wants Mass to be an important part of our life.
- How can we make people in church, especially guests, feel more welcome?
- What can we do to help others better appreciate that at Mass we share in the sacrifice of Christ on the cross and in his resurrection to glory?
- Without the Resurrection, the Eucharist has no meaning, just as suffering makes no sense. What does this mean to you in your life, right now?
- When friends or family members are troubled or in doubt, how can we encourage them to spend time in church praying for assistance from Christ, who is really present in the Eucharist?
- Meditate on the Eucharist as the real body and blood of Christ, who created the universe, sustains it, and dwells within our bodies in Holy Communion. How does

this realization help you appreciate the dignity of your body and those of others?

- What can we do to prepare ourselves, our family, and our loved ones to appreciate that when we receive Communion, we receive the real Christ?

- What does it mean to say that the Eucharist is the gateway for God's life-giving streams of grace to flow from the life-giving effects of Jesus' death and resurrection into the Church, the Body of Christ?

- How can we better realize that the Mass is the chief way that we show our thanks and praise to God, and that we go to Mass to do so, not only to pray for ourselves?

- What do you see as the relationship between effective proclamation of the Word and good liturgical music to the development of a more vibrant Christian community at Sunday Mass?

- What steps can we take to appreciate better that Christ's sacrifice on the cross is celebrated on the altar and that we participate in his sacrifice?

- What does it mean to say that the Eucharist is a sacrament of forgiveness? How can we better appreciate that the Eucharist is a sacrament for the forgiveness of venial sins, if we are truly sorry for them?

꙳

CHAPTER FIVE

❧

Reconciliation

Gateway to Healing of the Soul, to Deeper Union With God, and to the Ongoing Process of Conversion

TIRED AND FRUSTRATED, I RETURNED HOME from the office about 7:30 p.m. As I entered the kitchen to eat, Bruce, a pastoral worker, greeted me. He said that a depressed young man named Josh sat in the waiting room. He was not Catholic.

Shortly before I arrived, Josh rang the doorbell and asked for the pastor, saying that he was from Detroit. When learning that the pastor was not there, he requested a Bible, sackcloth, and ashes, the traditional symbols of penance.

Bruce asked if I would see him. I told Bruce to send him into the kitchen. Josh came in and sat at the table. He said little, refused to eat anything, and kept repeating that he was fasting and doing penance. As time passed, he became more depressed and asked again for a Bible, sackcloth, and ashes. He became upset when Bruce told him that we didn't have any ashes and sackcloth. I asked Josh if a dark sweater would do. He said yes, so Bruce got him a Bible and a dark sweater.

Eventually, Josh said he had to leave. It was cold outside. When learning he had nowhere to stay, I offered to find him overnight shelter. He declined and left. Ten minutes later he returned, saying, "It's cold out there."

He resumed his place at the table. I asked again if he wanted something to eat and offered him orange juice. He asked, "Will it break my fast?" I smiled and said no. He grabbed the pitcher of juice and drank most of it.

As I finished eating, Josh said practically nothing. Finally, he left through the front door. I was relieved but sad, wondering what was going on with this young man. When the pastor returned, I told him the episode and then went to my room, exhausted and puzzled.

Josh's guilt was apparent; what caused it, I didn't know.

A pounding on my door about 6:30 the next morning awoke me. It was the pastor, who then asked if I had let Josh back into the house during the night. After I said no, he asked: "How did he get back in? Did he have a key?" I was just as puzzled as the pastor was. He continued: "Several minutes ago, I walked through the downstairs hall and tripped over him, as he slept near the front door. There were no open doors or windows."

I dressed quickly and tried to talk to Josh. He stared forward with a blank glaze, depressed and bewildered, but said nothing. Feeling powerless, I called a social worker, who got nowhere with him. The social worker then called the police.

When two officers came up the front walk toward the door, Josh sat up, saying: "Thank goodness, maybe now I can have some peace. I killed a man yesterday and have been running ever since." We never heard any more about Josh, after the officers took him away in handcuffs.

I still wonder who Josh was. He showed guilt unlike anyone I had ever seen before. He must have been aware of the evil of sin, reflected in his remorse, as he asked for sackcloth and ashes. Why, when, and how he killed the man, I'll never know.

Josh's story shows how God builds into us the need for repentance. He gives us a conscience, the inner voice that tells us the difference between right and wrong. The Holy Spirit encourages us to do good, warns us of impending wrong, and urges us to avoid it. If we sin, our conscience calls us to repentance.

Reconciliation takes many forms, one of which is illustrated by Josh's guilt. The sacrament of Reconciliation is the gateway to healing the soul, creating a deeper union with God, and building ongoing conversion.

Reconciliation as a Gateway

Reconciliation (or Penance), a sacrament of mercy, is a consoling sacrament. Early Christians regarded it as a "second Baptism." Just as Baptism is the gateway to God's new life, bringing oneness with Christ and bestowing the grace of the Holy Spirit, so Reconciliation is the gateway to renewed life after we sin. It guarantees us that God forgives our sins through the absolution of the priest, as long as we are contrite and resolve to avoid the sin in the future. When mortal sin burdens the soul, absolution opens the floodgates of God's mercy. Then the person returns to the path of salvation and can receive Communion.

This sacrament invites us to refocus our lives. The *Catechism of the Catholic Church* says:

> Interior repentance is a radical reorientation of our whole life, a return, a conversion to God with all our heart, an end of sin, a turning away from evil, with repugnance toward the evil actions we have committed. At the same time, it entails the desire and resolution to change one's life. . . . (CCC 1431)

The sacrament of Reconciliation involves more than wishing to change our external actions. It requires us to make a sincere effort to change our hearts and a firm desire to avoid future sin.

Other kinds of penance — like prayer, fasting, and giving alms — also move us to conversion. Commitment to the poor, outreach to the sick, charitable works, justice, spiritual direction, suffering, and frequent confession also enhance our inner conversion and turn us away from sin.

History of Reconciliation

The need for reconciliation is as old as the human race. Chapter three of Genesis describes the fall of Adam and Eve and their punishment, as God drove them from the Garden. Other ancient creation stories reflect a similar theme. Those who wrote these accounts recognized that something is not right with our nature and that something must have occurred, causing the human race to stray from the right path. They also realized the need for rituals of forgiveness to express their repentance in words and deeds.

The Old Testament describes Jewish unfaithfulness, God's covenant, and his forgiveness. God seals his forgiveness with several covenants made between himself and the Jewish people. The Scriptures often describe Jewish unfaithfulness and their expressions of sorrow (with fasts, almsgiving, or sacrifices), and God's forgiveness.

Isaiah, Psalms, and other Old Testament books reflect this dynamic. Psalm 60, a communal psalm of Lament, says:

> O God, you have rejected us, broken
>   our defenses:
>   you have been angry, now restore us!
> . . . You have made your people suffer hard
>   things;
>   you have given us wine to drink that
>   made us reel.

Give victory with your right hand, and
    answer us,
  so that those whom you love may be
    rescued. (Ps 60:1, 3, 5)

Prayers of praise for God's wonderful works often accompanied requests for forgiveness. Old Testament patterns carried over into the early Church. In *Making Confession, Hearing Confession,* Annemarie Kidder writes: "In the New Testament the cycle of confession of sin, divine deliverance, and gratitude and praise persists."[16]

The Gospel narratives describe John the Baptist's preaching of repentance for the forgiveness of sins. He ritualized the penitent's conversion by a water rite of baptism in the Jordan River. John baptized Jesus when the Lord began his public life, even though he was free from sin.

The Old Testament considers sin as missing the mark or as a twisted, distorted condition. This same imagery continues in the New Testament.

Jesus moves beyond the external acts of sinners and focuses on their inner conversion. He forgave the woman caught in adultery and instructed her to sin no more (Jn 8:3-11). This involved changing her attitudes, not merely the cessation of sinful actions.

Jesus preached repentance and forgave sinners, depicted in the accounts of the paralytic lowered through the roof into Jesus' midst (Mk 2:1-12; also Mt 9:1-8 and Lk 5:17-26) and the woman caught in adultery, as cited above.

In Christian context, the historical and theological development of the sacrament of Reconciliation shows a similar concern for faith and conversion, as do the sacraments of initiation. During apostolic times, the change of life and the graces of Baptism were intended to set one's course for life without any "backsliding."[17] The problem arose when Christians sinned.

Early Christians, expecting Jesus' imminent Second Coming, believed that they would never again sin seriously. When Jesus did not come again quickly, and they did sin, the Church faced the problem of how to deal with those who fell into serious sin after Baptism. If repentant, should they be forgiven and included again in the community?

The Christian community considered ways to forgive sinners. The Eucharist was the ordinary way to ask forgiveness of venial sins. The Church also recommended prayer, fasting, and good works to forgive sins and their punishment, especially when praying the Our Father in the Eucharistic Prayer.

But what about more serious sins? In the second century, the *Shepherd of Hermas* mentioned a one-time reconciliation for those who fell into grave sin after Baptism. Others took a more rigorous position for the sins of adultery, murder, and apostasy. Some even considered them unforgivable sins.

Christian rituals played an important role in developing ways to forgive grave sins, like murder, apostasy, and adultery. Tertullian, in the early third century, wrote of a standard ritual to acknowledge the person as an official penitent. It included an expression of sorrow for sin, fasting, wearing penitential clothing, begging for the community's intercession, imposition of works of penance, public support of the prayers of the faithful, and eventual reconciliation with the Church.[18] Origen gives "seven ways of obtaining forgiveness: Baptism, martyrdom, almsgiving, forgiveness of others, conversion of sinners, and great love."[19] Then, he lists Reconciliation (Penance) as the seventh and most difficult way.

By the third century, the bishop assumed oversight of the process of Reconciliation. As an example of the bishop's role, Bishop Cyprian of Carthage denied pardons given by anyone else and insisted that it was the bishop's role to grant pardons for grave (mortal) sins.[20]

Grave sins, especially apostasy (repudiation of the Christian faith), occasioned the need to ask if such sins could be forgiven, and if repentant penitents could return to the Christian community. Eventually, the Church moved to public penances.

Public penance imposed on the penitent often required years to fulfill. When completed, the imposition of the bishop's hands on the penitent symbolized forgiveness, reunification with the Church, and the penitent's acceptance back into full communion with the Christian community.

By the fourth century, public penance was widespread but varied from place to place. After the Church judged the sin's seriousness, the penance imposed involved great austerity from the penitent. Penitents performed difficult acts of penance, like prolonged fasts, often dressed in sackcloth (coarse, rough clothing), and were forbidden to receive Communion.

The Church accepted the penitents back on Holy Thursday, after they completed their penance. If they fell into grave sin again, they could not repeat the process but instead had to throw themselves on God's mercy. Because of difficulties associated with public penance, its practice waned, and by the sixth century it was practically nonexistent.

Gradually, individual, or private, confession replaced public penances as the ordinary way to seek reconciliation for mortal sin. This repeatable practice of private confession and reconciliation eventually replaced all traces of the practice of public penance.

Many historians trace the origin of private confession to as early as the third century, when penitents began going into the desert to seek counsel from hermits and hermitesses (women hermits) living there. This counsel took on a penitential flavor. These early desert fathers and mothers influenced Irish missionaries, who took this practice with them to Ireland and other Celtic lands.

Private confession itself evolved in Ireland. Its beginnings there can be traced to the practice whereby some monks, unfaithful to the monastic rule and wishing to repent, went to the abbot of the monastery and asked for forgiveness. The abbot required them to do penances before rejoining the other monks and receiving Communion.

This practice spread beyond the monastery, and ordinary Christians sought out the abbot and other monks for counsel and support. This began a ritual of repeatable private confession, similar to what the monks did in the monastery. The people accepted it because of its confidentiality, ease in reception, and its leniency. In time, repeatable private confession spread to continental Europe.

By the thirteenth century, private confession was well established. St. Thomas Aquinas set the foundation for the theology of Reconciliation, which the Church adopted ever since. The penitent's outward signs of sorrow — contrition and confession — signified interior sorrow, brought about by God's grace. As this practice grew, the Fourth Lateran Council (1215) decreed that a person must confess at least once a year, if guilty of mortal sin, and that a person in mortal sin must go to confession before receiving Holy Communion. This requirement shows that the official Church not only accepted repeatable penance but counted on it.

During the Middle Ages, most priests heard confessions in public spots, since the confessional box did not appear until the sixteenth century. Manuals gave directions on how to hear confessions, the order of procedure, and the need for a penitent to make a complete confession of all mortal sins. Priests were instructed to take special care in hearing women's confessions, lest suspicion develop.

The Reformers, especially Martin Luther and John Calvin, objected to Church teachings and practices surrounding the sacrament of Reconciliation. Luther denied the need to go to a priest and to make a complete confession. Although he didn't deny entirely the value of Reconciliation, his views cut at the heart of Catholic belief regarding this sacrament. Calvin attacked Reconciliation's biblical basis.

Addressing the challenges of the Reformers, the Council of Trent reaffirmed the Catholic teachings on this sacrament and condemned those who attacked the Church's position. St. Ignatius Loyola defended the Church's traditional approach to Reconciliation, pointing out that it was a complicated process, developed during centuries of discussion, debate, and pastoral reflections.

In 1614, the Church decreed that a screen be put between the penitent and the priest. The Seal of Confession was also introduced at about this time. After Trent, the Church introduced few changes into the celebration of the sacrament, prior to Vatican II.

Before Vatican II, many Catholics went to confession weekly. Long lines of penitents sought absolution for their sins. Confession could be quite legalistic, and Catholics often confessed their sins to alleviate their guilt.

In the open atmosphere introduced by Pope John XXIII, the Second Vatican Council reformed the sacrament of Reconciliation, following a similar pattern used with other sacraments.

In 1973, the Sacred Congregation for Divine Worship issued new rites and norms for Reconciliation.

It decreed three rites: one for the absolution of single penitents; the second, a communal rite for a larger group of penitents, requiring individual confession and absolution for each one; and the third for large numbers of penitents, with general confession and absolution in times of necessity. The third rite required strict conditions for its use. It said that if penitents have committed mortal sins, those sins are forgiven through general confession, but also stipulated that those sins must be confessed later to a priest in individual confession.

In the second (or communal) rite, the assembly gathers, sings, hears God's Word that encourages repentance, and listens to the priest's homily. A communal examination of conscience often accompanies this celebration. At the appropriate time, the priest or several priests take their places in various spots in church and hear individual confessions, give spiritual advice, absolve the penitents, and give penances.

Vatican II ushered in other changes. In the individual rite, the priest and penitent could now sit face-to-face for confession, if the penitent wished. The Church encourages the priest to take a pastoral approach and avoid the former legalism. He greets the penitent, reads from Scripture, and encourages the penitent to be sorry and to confess sins. Then the priest gives spiritual advice, bestows a penance, and absolves the individual.

Being Catholic is a way of life. Regular confession helps us to stay on the right path, to grow in faith, and to mature as Catholics. Having a regular confessor can be a great help in doing so.

Today, the reception of the sacrament of Reconciliation is rare or nonexistent for many Catholics. The long lines of penitents waiting to receive this sacrament are gone. The reasons are multiple and complex, but suffice it to say that the current trend is unfortunate. Catholics need to learn to appreciate Reconciliation as a sacrament that helps them to avoid sin, to lead a good life, and to grow in grace.

When we sin, we offend God, ourselves, and those who suffer because of our sins. The sacrament of Reconciliation is an opportunity for renewal and comfort.

Basic Church Teachings on Reconciliation

Sin is a deliberate offense against God. It can be a willful thought, word, desire, action, or omission against God's law. It violates the love of God and neighbor, going against the basic Christian commandment given by Jesus to love God above all things and to love our neighbor as our self.

When we sin, we choose ourselves and sinful pleasures over God and his people. Mortal (deadly) sin permanently ruptures our union with God. Reconciliation requires sincere sorrow and inner conversion. Since sin offends God and wounds our relationship with the Church, it necessitates reconciliation with God and the ecclesial community.

Only God can forgive sins. When Jesus founded his Church, he bestowed on her the special power to forgive sins in his name. He told Peter, "I will give you the keys of the kingdom of heaven, and whatever you bind on earth will be bound in heaven, and whatever you loose on earth will be loosed in heaven" (Mt 16:19). Through these words, Jesus entrusted this power to Peter and his successors. As the *Catechism of the Catholic Church* puts it, "he entrusted the exercise of the power of absolution to the apostolic ministry which he charged with the 'ministry of reconciliation' (2 Cor 5:18)" (CCC 1442). Being reconciled with God is the first step toward healing the wounds of sin. In the sacrament of Reconciliation, the priest forgives in the name of the Trinity.

The Church, through the authority of the pope and bishops, determines which sins exclude us from Holy Communion. She also establishes penalties, like excommunication and suspension, for extremely serious sins.

As baptized followers of Jesus, Christians reflect God's forgiveness by their willingness to forgive those who have offended them.

Liturgically, God's forgiveness comes through the sacraments of Baptism, the Eucharist, Reconciliation (Penance), and the Anointing of the Sick, each in different ways. Baptism remits original sin. It also forgives all mortal and venial sins committed before its reception, if the one baptized is truly sorry.

The Eucharist is a sacrament of reconciliation. Here we celebrate the dying and rising of Jesus that opened the floodgates of God's mercy, love, and forgiveness, previously blocked by Adam's sin. The Eucharist forgives venial sins. If a person has sinned mortally, he or she must confess mortal sins in the sacrament of Reconciliation before receiving Holy Communion.

The sacrament of Reconciliation is "above all for those who, since Baptism, have fallen into grave sin, and have thus lost their baptismal grace and wounded ecclesial communion" (CCC 1446). The Church encourages all baptized Catholics to receive this sacrament to grow in grace and avoid sin.

The sacrament of Reconciliation gives peace and comfort to sinners, especially those who sin gravely. It's easy to appreciate this marvelous sacrament, if we consider the alternative. If there were no sacrament of Reconciliation, could we be as confident that God has forgiven us?

The bishops (and the priests commissioned by the bishops, religious superiors, or the pope, according to Church law) exercise the ministry of Reconciliation (CCC 1462). They act in the person of Christ as healers and reconcilers, urging sinners to repent and begin a new life. They are bound by the strictest law of the Church never to reveal what has been confessed in the sacrament of Reconciliation. This is known as the "Seal of Confession," for whatever is confessed remains forever sealed in the soul of the confessor. Priests have gone to their death by refusing to violate the Seal of Confession.

When Jesus forgave sins, he required the sinner's conversion before forgiving the sin. The same thing is true today. The acts of the penitent include contrition, confession, a firm resolve not to commit the sin again, and satisfaction (doing penance for the sins). To deepen our conversion, the priest in the sacrament of Reconciliation prays with us and assigns a penance, prior to absolving our sins. If the penitent is sorry, God's forgiveness happens through the priest's absolution. Forgiveness requires divine action on God's part and penitential acts on our part.

The Church distinguishes between perfect and imperfect contrition. Perfect contrition is sorrow for our sins mainly because they offend the all-good and loving God. Imperfect contrition is true sorrow, motivated primarily by fear of God's punishment for our sins. For example, if a person knowingly and willingly commits intentional murder, this is a grievous offense against God and a mortal sin. If later he is sorry and asks for God's forgiveness mainly because his sin was a serious sin against God, whom he loves above all things, his sorrow can have no greater motive. He seriously offended God and did violence to his neighbor, but now his love is selfless and as perfect as a human being can have. This is perfect contrition. If, however, the person is truly sorry, but mainly because of fear of God's punishment (including eternity in hell), his sorrow is genuine, but his motive is imperfect. This is imperfect contrition.

Perfect contrition forgives all sins, but we must confess our mortal sins before receiving Holy Communion. Imperfect contrition does not forgive mortal sins by itself, but imperfect contrition *and* the absolution given by the priest in the sacrament of Reconciliation forgive mortal sins.

The sacrament of Reconciliation returns the sinner in mortal sin to God's grace. It confers sanctifying grace on the penitent and reestablishes the friendship between God and the sinner, lost by mortal sin. It also confers actual graces to help avoid sin in the future. Those in venial sin receive actual graces to grow in God's love and to break or diminish sinful habits.

The sacrament of Reconciliation also remits some temporal punishment in purgatory for the sins forgiven. It helps a penitent deepen his or her ongoing conversion, leading to greater love of God and service of neighbor.

Reconciliation and Basic Human Needs

Our basic needs move us to strive for peace and inner harmony and to stay on the right path. The sacrament of Reconciliation addresses these needs.

From the dawn of creation, people wondered why strife and evil exist. The second creation story

(Gen 2:4-3:24) addresses evil in the world and points to the original sin of Adam and Eve as its cause. Evil entered the world with original sin. From this time, an evil or sinful condition existed. The effects of this sin permeate our inner being and incline us to sin. Our personal sins ratify or make this sinful condition worse.

Although war and strife are part of our human condition, a deeper desire for stability and peace exists. Without inner peace, chaos and strife disturb the harmony necessary for our personal and communal growth.

The devastating effects of broken marriages or a war-weary country are all around us. When worries beset us and we cannot sleep, this affects us. Sin also disturbs our equilibrium. Faced with weakness, the temptations of life, and the influence of the devil, we sometimes sin. Sins disrupt our inner balance and bring us guilt and shame. We desire peace but have no peace. We desire to be forgiven so that we can resume our growth and move toward ultimate salvation. The sacrament of Reconciliation is an important way to have our sins forgiven and to satisfy our need for peace. To do so, we must stay on the right path. Getting off of it causes us grief and worry.

Once, while taking a hike in an isolated forest, a friend and I walked for miles on what we thought was a footpath. Then it ceased, and we realized that it was no more than an animal trail. We wondered what we should do. Instead of returning the way we came, we decided to venture farther into the forest, in a direction that we thought would lead us to a road. We walked and walked, once in a circle, not sure where we were, as we moved deeper into the forest.

We were lost.

As daylight turned to dusk, our fear intensified, but we kept going. Eventually, we found a small river and followed it, hoping it would lead us to a town. When darkness descended, we saw a car light. It wasn't a town but instead a road that led us to safety.

As I think about this incident, I think of the need to stay on the right path in the spiritual sense. When we are tempted to do wrong, it's easy to take the wrong path and get lost in a mire of wrongdoing. When this happens, something within moves us to regain our equilibrium and return to the right path. When confused or lost in the midst of sinful actions, we may be on no path, wandering lost through the "forest," as my friend and I did, before we found the road.

When lost, we search for a way out. We sometimes seek advice from parents, friends, or professional counselors to help us find a way out of our confusion, returning to our original path and resuming righteous living.

God put into us the desire to reestablish equilibrium after we sin. This happens when we are sorry for our sins and repent. The sacrament of Reconciliation is Jesus' gift to allow this to happen.

Receiving absolution is not the same as being counseled. Counseling helps those who need advice, are troubled, or struggle with guilt. The sacrament of Reconciliation is the answer, if we have sinned and are guilty of moral failures. It assures us that God forgives us, if we are sorry and ask for his mercy. To regain interior peace, we need God's help, and the peace that comes with his forgiveness.

࿇

COMMUNAL AND PERSONAL IMPLICATIONS

What implications can we draw from this chapter on Reconciliation for a better understanding and more fruitful participation in this sacrament?

The sacrament of Reconciliation offers us the opportunity to regularly examine our conscience and to ask ourselves how we are fulfilling Jesus' call to follow him. This is a time to recognize the consequences of living the life of Christ and the need to grow in virtue. Being another Christ has different meanings for a mother, a father, a child, a businessman, a doctor, a nurse, an executive, or a laborer.

Confession invites us to accept our Christian responsibilities. For the teenager, this may mean asking: "Are my provocative clothes the kind that a follower of Christ should wear?" or "Are the girls or guys that I hang around with good for me, or do they lead me into wrong behavior?" or "Does a follower of Christ act as I do, when I smoke pot or drink too much?" For the adult, this may mean asking: "Is this business practice proper for a follower of Christ?" or "Is my moral behavior acceptable?"

Reconciliation challenges us to say no to sin and to avoid the near occasions of sin. Followers of Christ root out bad habits that prevent them from imitating him and develop good habits that bring them closer to God.

Take a few moments to reflect on the above comments on the sacrament of Reconciliation or on those listed below:

- How does making an examination of conscience on a regular basis and asking for forgiveness in this sacrament help us eradicate or lessen our sins?
- How does regular confession help us grow in virtue and relate better to family members?
- Discuss with your spouse or family the value of the sacrament of Reconciliation, as it pertains to family relationships.
- Learn more about the history of the sacrament of Reconciliation, and check a Catholic bookstore, your parish library, or the Catholic literature rack at church to see what Catholic resources on this

subject might help you. If possible, attend a workshop or lecture centering on this sacrament.

- Check for communal celebrations of the sacrament of Reconciliation at your parish or at a neighboring one, and make an effort to attend them.
- The Eucharist ritualizes God's forgiveness of venial sins. What does that mean to you and your life?
- Prayer, fasting, and good works for the forgiveness of daily sins also help us avoid sin in the future. How does this give you confidence in God's love for you?
- Reflect on the fact that sin disrupts our inner sense of balance, and that we feel guilt and shame. When this happens, we desire peace but have no peace. Apply this to your life, especially to regular habits of sinning.
- When we sin, we choose ourselves and sinful pleasures over God and his people. Mortal (deadly) sin permanently ruptures our union with God. How does this apply to your life?
- In the sacrament of Reconciliation, God forgives our sins through the absolution of the priest, as long as we are sorry for

our sins and resolve to avoid the sins in the future. What does this say about the value of receiving the sacrament of Reconciliation frequently to help us overcome sinful habits?

- If you are in a parish adult-formation group, ask the participants to give their opinions as to why many people have stopped receiving the sacrament of Reconciliation or receive it rarely. If you are not in such a group, consider joining one. If there is not a group, ask parish leaders to begin one.

෨

CHAPTER SIX

ॐ

Anointing of the Sick

Gateway to Renewed Health Here and Eternal Life Hereafter

THE FIRST TIME I ENTERED the Home for the Aged, shortly after my ordination, it was about 6:30 in the morning. The year was 1960, and the Church required fasting and abstinence beginning at midnight for those who received Holy Communion. Those living there needed to receive Communion before they ate breakfast.

I walked into the dark corridor adjoining the furnace room in the basement on my way to the first floor. As I went around the corner, a thin trembling arm came out of the darkness and reached for me. I jumped back, not knowing what was happening.

In the blackness, an old lady sat in a wheelchair. She remained silent but trembled in an attempt to reach out and contact another human being. Every week thereafter she was there, saying nothing but touching my arm as I walked past her on my way upstairs to distribute Communion to four people.

I brought Communion upstairs to Margaret, Bessie, Ann, and Chester. Margaret had been confined to her bed for twenty-two years and never had a visitor. Ann, a semi-paralyzed forty-year-old, showed me pictures of her relatives, but she told me they were too busy to visit her. Bessie rarely spoke.

When Bessie died, I went to the funeral home to bless her and console the family. As I arrived, the undertaker greeted me with the words, "I'm really glad you came." Examining the visitors' book, I saw that I was her only visitor. The next morning at the funeral Mass, I welcomed her body and celebrated the Eucharist with only the undertaker. Even the servers and singers forgot to come.

My clearest memories of the Home for the Aged are of Chester, an old man living on the third floor. During one visit, he said that he wanted to be anointed and receive Viaticum (Communion given when approaching death) before he died. When I was called to anoint him, Chester was in a deep coma and near death. The nurse said he was unable to receive Communion. Seeing him, I realized that he already had begun his journey to God. I anointed him and hoped to give him Viaticum. I asked him if he could hear me. There was no answer. Then, I put my hand into his frail hands and said, "Chester, this is your friend, Father Bob. If you understand me and want to receive Holy Communion as you go to God, press on my hand."

As if from a faraway place, I felt a faint pressing on my hand. After it happened again, I knew that

Chester had heard me. When giving him Viaticum, I took a spoon, put a sliver of host in water, and gently poured it down his throat. Chester received his final wish on his journey to eternal life.

It's been fifty years since that time, but the memories of anointing him and giving him Communion are still vivid.

Times have changed. This sacrament is no longer administered only to dying people. Today, we call it the Anointing of the Sick rather than Extreme Unction (Last Rites). It is the gateway to health here and eternal life hereafter. It heals the soul and sometimes the body, and it unites us to Jesus in his suffering and death.

The Anointing of the Sick as a Gateway

A gateway opens up new possibilities. The Anointing of the Sick is a gateway to spiritual, emotional, and physical healing. It strengthens the sick and prepares the dying to enter eternal life. It bestows spiritual healing on broken people, brings peace and emotional support, and forgives sins. We celebrate life transitions through rites of passage that ritualize changes from one state of life to another. Anointing celebrates the passage from sickness to health, or from death to eternal life.

I witnessed the spiritual and emotional effects of anointing when a nurse called around midnight and asked me to come to a retirement home. An unconscious elderly woman hung onto life. Her daughter said that her mother wanted to be anointed. After I anointed her, a great inner peace came over her, and she died an hour later.

Anointing sometimes brings physical healing. I anointed Martha, an elderly woman, at her home about six times in two years. On each occasion, the doctor said she would not live, but she did. Once, the doctor said: "Father, I don't know what you do with that oil, for I am not Catholic. Martha should have died two years ago. She will not live this time." A month later, her son asked me to bring her Holy Communion. When I arrived, the elderly woman held the paint bucket, as her son painted the living room. Martha was still alive when I left the parish.

History of the Anointing of the Sick

The Anointing of the Sick has a rich history, beginning with Jesus' curing the sick and forgiving sins. He gave this power to the Church. Key historical points help us appreciate the value of this sacrament.

Sick people often ask God for help. Throughout history, various cultures have used oil as a healing remedy. Ancient Egyptians and Greeks used olive oil to treat wounds and reduce fever. They rubbed athletes with oil after strenuous workouts or to prepare their bodies for competition. They also used aromatic oils and expensive spikenard oil, the kind that tradition says the penitent woman used to anoint Jesus' feet. The Jews anointed kings, priests, and prophets with oil. They used it to cure wounds and soothe the sick.

Old Testament Jews recognized God as the master of life and death. When ill, they sought his help. They believed that sickness could lead to conversion, which began when they begged God for forgiveness. Isaiah says that in the new kingdom, God will forgive sins and heal every kind of illness (Is 33:24).

The New Testament shows Jesus' love for the sick and dying. He cured the blind man, the paralytic, the woman with an issue of blood, and Lazarus. He went about the countryside, using visible signs, like the laying on of his hands, to forgive sins and heal various kinds of illness. His healing actions prefigure the Church's use of visible signs to heal and forgive.

Jesus healed the entire person — body, soul, and spirit (Mk 2:17). His disciples also healed people. As Mark says, "They cast out many demons, and anointed with oil many who were sick and cured them" (Mk 6:13). At the Last Judgment, Jesus told us that whatever we do for the sick, we do for him (Mt 25:36). He showed us that spiritual healing is deeper than physical healing, as he heals us from sin and death by his death on the cross.

The *Catechism of the Catholic Church* says, "By his passion and death on the cross Christ has given

a new meaning to suffering: it can henceforth con-
figure us to him and unite us with his redemptive
Passion" (CCC 1505). The Church continues Jesus'
healing ministry through visible signs like priestly
absolution in Reconciliation and anointing with oil
in the Anointing of the Sick.

After he ascended into heaven, Jesus sent the
Holy Spirit on Pentecost to enable his Church to
be the prime mediator of God's healing. Following
Christ's command, the early Church developed a rite
of healing for the sick and dying that the Letter of
James describes:

> Are any among you sick? They should call
> for the elders of the church and have them
> pray over them, anointing them with oil in
> the name of the Lord. The prayer of faith will
> save the sick, and the Lord will raise them
> up; and anyone who has committed sins will
> be forgiven. (Jas 5:14-15)

James stresses the significance of faith for healing and connects forgiveness with healing. This ho-
listic perspective involves the entire person. In *Understanding the Sacraments Today*, Lawrence Mick
writes: "In the first eight hundred years, the sacrament was clearly seen as a rite for the sick."[21] The
Anointing of the Sick was part of the Church's ordinary healing ministry. The presbyters anointed the
sick with oil blessed by the bishop.

Differences existed regarding who administered this sacrament. From the early Church until the ninth century, the Latin Church and some Eastern Catholic Churches permitted the laity to bestow a lay anointing, as they took the oil blessed by the bishop to the sick. This was analogous to how they brought the Eucharist to the sick as well. Clerical anointing was the norm in some places, especially in Rome. Venerable Bede, an English scholar and saint living in the eighth century, mentions both forms of anointing.

Charlemagne dictated a reformed liturgy for his reign as Holy Roman emperor in the ninth century. He adapted clerical anointing, the rite of anointing practiced in Rome. Anointing became associated with the sacrament of Penance (Reconciliation), especially in the Carolingian period (around the years 800-1000), and eventually it was restricted to the clergy. This has been the practice in the Western (Latin) Church ever since.

The sacrament also shifted focus from a sacrament for the sick to a sacrament for the dying, known as "Extreme Unction" (for the dying). The Eastern Catholic Churches never referred to it as Extreme Unction. The Council of Trent adopted a middle road, saying that "the sacrament was to be administered to the sick, especially to those who were dangerously ill and seemed near death."[22]

The Council of Trent stressed that Extreme Unction is a sacrament, in opposition to the Protestant reformers who denied this.

Vatican II focused the sacrament on the sick but said that it is to be administered especially to the dying. The sacrament of Extreme Unction was renamed the Anointing of the Sick. Many modifications accompanied this new orientation, including a new liturgical rite in which the priest may anoint the sick and elderly in a communal setting or in individual anointing, often at a Eucharistic celebration. Today, this sacrament gives strength and consolation to the sick, to the dying, and to their loved ones.

Basic Church Teachings on the Anointing of the Sick

We instinctively try to avoid sickness, an inevitable part of life. Faced with it, we may feel dread, anguish, and near despair, and faith may be our only consolation.

I experienced such feelings during a prolonged illness forty years ago. No one, including the doctors, knew what caused me to lose my strength, as my body steadily deteriorated and my spirit waned. As Easter approached, sitting alone in my room, a deep anguish came over me. The pain was so intense that I began beating my head on the wall, hoping to lessen my anxiety. I kept asking, "Why?" Frustrated and with little hope, I turned my head to the wall and noticed the crucifix hanging there. Then I thought, "If you made it, so can I." Thoughts of my union with Christ strengthened me and gave me the determination to go on.

This perception didn't remove my pain, but it enabled me to endure it. Later, when I recovered, I realized that this was a turning point in my life. It gave me the insight needed to grow into a mature Christian. Afterward, my search for God and life's ultimate meaning were more than words in a book. They became a lived reality in my daily activities.

The Second Vatican Council puts it this way: "By the sacred anointing of the sick and the prayer of the priests the whole Church commends those who are ill to the suffering and glorified Lord that he may raise them up and save them."[23] These words put the sick person into the Lord's hands and join their sufferings to Christ's suffering and resurrection.

Jesus healed the sick, and the Church continues his healing ministry. Anointing is administered to the seriously ill, the aged, those undergoing surgery, and the dying.

The Council of Trent said:

This reality [that is, the reality signified by this sacrament] is in fact the grace of the Holy Spirit, whose anointing takes away sins, if any still remain to be taken away, and the remnants of sin; [this anointing] also relieves and strengthens the soul of the sick person, arousing . . . a great confidence in the divine

mercy, whereby . . . [the person] more easily
bears the trials and labors of [the] sickness,
. . . and sometimes regains bodily health, if
this is expedient for the health of the soul.[24]

This sacrament gives the sick person grace to re-
sist attacks from the evil one and to grow in union
with Christ's Paschal Mystery. It may be repeated
during a new serious illness or in a significant dete-
riorating condition in the same illness.

*Pastoral Care of the Sick: Rites of Anointing and
Viaticum* encourages the sick person to receive the
sacrament of Reconciliation before being anointed
and receiving Communion. The rite says, "If it is
necessary for the sick person to confess during the
celebration of the sacrament of anointing, this takes
the place of the penitential rite" (n. 113).

The Anointing of the Sick brings many blessings
to the sick person. The *Catechism of the Catholic
Church* lists the following:

- "*A particular gift of the Holy Spirit*" (CCC 1520;
  emphasis in original). This sacrament gives
  us courage, peace, and strength to endure and
  conquer the hard times that accompany serious
  sickness.

- "*Union with the passion of Christ*" (CCC 1521;
  emphasis in original). Anointing joins our sufferings with those of Christ, enabling us to participate more fully in Jesus' redemptive death.

It also helps us see that Jesus has redeemed us from original sin, the source of human agony. In accepting our suffering in union with him, we join in the salvation of humankind. As the *Catechism of the Catholic Church* states, "The Anointing of the Sick completes our conformity to the death and Resurrection of Christ, just as Baptism began it. It completes the holy anointings that mark the whole Christian life: that of Baptism which sealed the new life in us, and that of Confirmation which strengthened us for the combat of this life" (CCC 1523).

• "*An ecclesial grace*" (CCC 1522; emphasis in original). As members of Christ's Mystical Body, the Anointing of the Sick invites all the living and the dead to intercede for the sick person.

• "*A preparation for the final journey*" (CCC 1523; emphasis in original). Anointing directs us toward our final suffering that prepares us for eternity. Joined to Christ in Baptism, we began our journey to God. Anointing prepares for the completion of this journey, as we ready ourselves to return to God in union with Jesus in his death and resurrection. Anointing fortifies the end of our lives "like a solid rampart for the final struggles before entering the Father's house" (CCC 1523).

The Anointing of the Sick shows life's frailty and puts it into perspective. It invites us to appreciate who we are and what we are called to become.

The Anointing of the Sick has several basic elements. These include the priest's praying for the sick person; the proclamation of Scripture; his laying on of hands upon the sick person; anointing the forehead and hands of the sick person with the duly blessed oil (pressed from olives or other plants); and saying only once the required sacramental form of anointing. When necessary, it is sufficient to anoint only the forehead or another part of the body. In ordinary circumstances, it is appropriate to say the first part of the form when anointing the forehead and the second part when anointing the hands.

Here is the sacramental form used in the Latin rite when anointing the person:

> Through this holy anointing
> may the Lord in his love and mercy help you
> with the grace of the Holy Spirit.
>
> May the Lord who frees you from sin
> save you and raise you up.[25]

Bishops and priests are ministers of this sacrament. Generally, the oil used is blessed by the bishop. In case of necessity, any priest can bless the oil "but only in the actual celebration of the sacrament" (CIC, c. 999, 2°).

The person being anointed must have the desire to receive it. If the person is unconscious, is in a coma, or has recently died and there is doubt whether the soul is still in the body, the sacrament can be administered conditionally. In this regard, the *Code of Canon Law* states, "This sacrament is to be administered in a case of doubt whether the sick person has attained the use of reason, is dangerously ill, or is dead" (CIC, c. 1005). Dead people have already made their journey to God and are not anointed. The question of whether death has occurred is sometimes not easy to determine.

Anointing of the Sick may take place individually or in a communal celebration. In the latter case, sick and elderly people are anointed in a communal ritual involving prayers and readings, often in church at Mass, in the presence of relatives, friends, and the community. In this celebration, the sick and the elderly listen to God's words, receive individual anointing, participate in the Eucharist, and praise God. They pray for physical, emotional, and spiritual healing together with the broader church community.

The Anointing of the Sick and Basic Human Needs

We have basic needs for health, wholeness, and an afterlife. The Anointing of the Sick addresses these needs.

The Christian belief that we live on after death gives us hope, which I have witnessed with many sick people before their death and with relatives after their loved ones died.

Belief in an afterlife is not an accident; it is rooted in the core of who we are. God created us with a built-in desire to live on. St. Augustine's famous phrase in his *Confessions* reflects this when he says that we are made for God alone, and that our hearts are restless until they rest in God.

Anointing of the Sick helps us to fulfill our need for wholeness and to complete our life cycle. We are born, grow, mature, reach adulthood, marry, have children, experience joy and sorrow, grow old, and die. Death breaks us out of our life cycle on earth and moves us to a new realm of being.

The goal of the Christian life is eternal happiness. Jesus assured us that our life reaches fulfillment through his Paschal Mystery. At death, we join Christ in eternal glory, the final reward for living in union with Jesus on earth. Anointing invites us into eternal life.

ॐ

COMMUNAL AND PERSONAL IMPLICATIONS

What implications can we draw from this chapter on the Anointing of the Sick for a better understanding and more fruitful participation in this sacrament?

Sickness often forces us to take another look at ourselves. The Anointing of the Sick reminds us of our finality, especially when we are sick or see a loved one suffer and die. Sickness is a time of transition, affording real opportunities for both the sick person and healthy loved ones.

When ministering to the sick, or if we are sick ourselves, it's important to see the Anointing of the Sick as focused on spiritual and physical health, not on death. Such a positive attitude helps us endure the pain, loneliness, and ambiguity that accompany sickness.

When a person is seriously ill, Catholics are to call the priest immediately and ask for the sacrament. Because of the HIPAA law (which contains government regulations concerning the privacy of individuals), hospitals cannot automatically inform parishes that a Catholic parishioner has been hospitalized, as was once the custom. Hospitals can only contact parishes if they receive specific permission from the patient to do so.

Before death, *prudent* words and actions from family members and visitors when in the presence of the seriously sick person are necessary. For example, once when I visited a dying person, those present were speaking of what to do after the person died. When I encouraged them to leave the room to talk about funeral arrangements, a relative said: "It doesn't make any difference; she's in a coma." He failed to realize that when someone is in a coma, often the last sense to cease functioning is hearing. Comatose people, considered by some visitors as unable to understand what is going on, may actually hear. Ample evidence of this comes from individuals who have returned to consciousness and said that they knew and heard what was going on while in a comatose state.

It's hard to imagine how a person, lying helpless and dying, feels when she or he hears someone making funeral arrangements. When administering the Anointing of the Sick, those present need to presume that the man or woman hears and understands what is going on as the anointing proceeds.

With this in mind, take a few moments to reflect on the above comments on the Anointing of the Sick or on those listed below:

- What does our belief in the afterlife say about our priorities and lifestyle?
- How do the following words of Scripture influence your attitude toward the sick? "The prayer of faith will save the sick, and the Lord will raise them up; and anyone who has committed sins will be forgiven" (Jas 5:15).
- Have you or a loved one experienced

suffering that changed your attitude toward life? Reflect on it, and if appropriate, discuss it with someone.

- Have you been anointed or have you been present when a person close to you was anointed? If so, how did you feel, and what was going on within you?
- Have you told your relatives that you wish to be anointed and to call the priest when you are seriously ill or in the hospital? If not, you may consider doing so.
- How do you feel that the Anointing of the Sick can help us endure the pain, loneliness, and ambiguity of ordinary life?
- How does the Anointing of the Sick join our sufferings with those of Christ, thus enabling us to participate more fully in Jesus' redemptive death?
- What can we do to help family members better appreciate the value of the Anointing of the Sick and to encourage them to come with us for a parish anointing ceremony?
- What steps can we take to encourage neighbors and other parishioners to call a priest to administer the Anointing of the Sick to dying people and those undergoing serious surgery?
- Jesus healed the sick, and the Church

continues his ministry through her healing ministry. When someone at home is
sick, point out to family members how
the Anointing of the Sick fits into the
Church's broader healing ministry.

- The Anointing of the Sick, a gateway
to spiritual and physical healing, gives
strength to the sick, asks for healing,
and prepares the dying to enter eternal
life. What does this mean to you?

CHAPTER SEVEN

∽

Matrimony

Gateway Affirming the Sacramentality of the Body and God's Love Reflected in the Mutual Love of the Spouses

OUR FAMILY HOME SPOKE OF MY PARENTS' LOVE, even though words like "Marriage between Christians is a covenant" were not part of their preparation for marriage. I learned of their wedding through stories, old photo albums, and wedding pictures. The photos depict them as young adults — going to Mt. Echo Park in Cincinnati and Clifty Falls near Madison, Indiana — having a great time with friends and family members. The pictures reflect their happiness on their wedding day. The family album also shows my sisters, brother, and me, as we grew up, left home, and matured. The fruit of their marriage resides in the flesh, blood, and spirit of my sisters and brother.

I remember the day that I took my parents on a ride through Dad's boyhood neighborhood, as his health declined. He retold the story of how he grew up, how he and Mom met, and how our family began.

Over the years, Mom sometimes mentioned an intelligent high-school classmate who received a senior-class college scholarship. But on this day, she revealed more. Mom said, "I got a scholarship." I asked her why she didn't accept it and go to college, for Mom was one of the smartest people I ever knew.

She smiled and said, "Bob, after my father died, we were quite poor." Then she went on to say: "Grandma had to work as a cleaning lady. We barely made ends meet with her income. When I returned home from school and told Grandma that I had received a four-year, all-paid college scholarship, she thought for moment and said, 'Olivia, we are too poor for you to go to college. We don't have the money to buy you the books and clothes you'll need. Go back to school, thank the sisters, and tell them you must work to help support our family.' "

Stunned at Mom's humility, I said nothing. She finally revealed her secret of selfless love that she had showed throughout her life. Then she added: "That was fine, Bob. If I had accepted the scholarship, I would not have met your father, and you would not be here today."

What more could I say, except, "Thanks, Mom"? From such selfless love on the part of my parents, I learned more about a loving marriage than from theology books, lectures, scholarly research, or pastoral reflections.

Matrimony is the gateway to the deepest relationship possible between a man and a woman. For Christians, this includes a new relationship with

Christ through one's spouse, the sharing of divine life in procreating children, and the reciprocal love of family members.

Matrimony as a Gateway

Christ describes his love for the Church in terms of marital love. Matrimony is a gateway opening up the depths of God's intimate love, reflected in the love of man and woman in marriage. It affirms the sacramentality of the body and God's love manifested in spousal love. The sacred act of intercourse brings to fulfillment the holiness present in other aspects of married life, which other sacraments reinforce and enhance.

Manifestations of God's presence in nature and human relationships reach their highest point in marriage. As a gateway, to reiterate what was said above, the sacrament of Matrimony affirms the sacramentality of the body and of God's love, reflected in the mutual love of spouses and their begetting of children. For Christians, these sacramental actions share in the sacramentality of Christ's love.

In the Old Testament, God entered a covenant with the Jewish people. In the New Testament, Jesus established a new covenant in his blood. Christian marriage participates in Jesus' covenant love in the love that a couple shares with each other. They continually renew this covenant throughout their married life.

While maintaining spousal self-identity and respect, Christian marriage is a sacrament that involves full cooperation with the other person. It draws its inspiration from Jesus' love and his sacrifice on the cross. Just as he lived a life of service, likewise spouses in a sacramental marriage serve others within and beyond their family. At times, marital service, the opposite of self-gratification, involves the offering of oneself for a spouse, children, and others. This self-sacrifice flows from the nature of the sacrament of Matrimony and is a way for Christians to live in imitation of Jesus. The dying to self required in marriage points to our connection with Christ, the man for others.

Often, no one outside of the family knows the heroic, unglamorous service performed by dedicated fathers or mothers. Here, faithful spouses fulfill their calling to be servants in imitation of Jesus.

Service to each other requires that spouses support each other. This helps those within and outside of the family to recognize the importance of Christian service. In such service, children first see a loving God through their parents.

History of Matrimony

Christian marriage has an uneven history, and the way it was celebrated varied greatly. Its history reveals a growing appreciation of this sacrament's dignity.

Genesis teaches that marriage originated with God's creation of man and woman, made in God's image (Gen 1:26-27). After the Fall, spousal disloyalty, unfaithfulness, polygamy, and other abuses often challenged this sacred union. Jewish leaders tolerated the polygamy of patriarchs and kings, while Mosaic Law prohibited a man's arbitrary domination of his wife (Deut 24:1-4).

The prophets prepared for a deeper appreciation of the unity and permanent character of the marital covenant (Hos 1-3 and Is 54 and 62). As the *Catechism of the Catholic Church* says, "The books of *Ruth* and *Tobit* bear moving witness to an elevated sense of marriage and to the fidelity and tenderness of spouses" (CCC 1611; emphasis in original). In this regard, the prophets sometimes compared God's love for Israel to the faithful love of a husband for his wife.

Jesus elevated marriage to the dignity of a sacrament. He performed his first public miracle at the marriage feast of Cana. The *Catechism of the Catholic Church* says, "She [the Church] sees in it [Jesus' presence at the wedding feast of Cana] the confirmation of the goodness of marriage and the proclamation that thenceforth marriage will be an efficacious sign of Christ's presence" (CCC 1613).

Jesus returned to the original nature of God's plan that one man and one woman be united in marriage. Matthew 19:6 says, "Therefore what God has joined together, let no one separate." Referring to marriage, the Letter to the Ephesians says:

> For this reason a man will leave his father
> and mother and be joined to his wife, and
> the two will become one flesh. This is a great
> mystery, and I am applying it to Christ and
> the church. (Eph 5:25-26, 31-32)

In this passage, St. Paul compares the oneness in marriage to the unity between Christ and his Church. Spousal unity and love, then, connect with the great mystery of the love between Jesus and his Mystical Body, the Church.

The early Church recognized the spirituality of Christian marriage, but it developed no special religious rituals to celebrate it. Rather, Christians followed the local customs for the celebration of marriage. As Lawrence Mick puts it, "For centuries the actual form of the marriage varied according to local customs and traditions."[26]

The difference, however, was that even though Christians used the same legal norms and followed the same marriage rituals as non-believers, Christians were "married in the Lord." Christians knew that their marriages were blessed by the Holy Spirit, and that Christian marriage reflected God's permanent and indissoluble covenant with the Church.

The practice of celebrating Christian marriages in religious liturgies became more widespread during the ninth century. By the Late Middle Ages, this became the accepted custom, although variations still existed. It wasn't until the Council of Trent that the Church no longer recognized clandestine marriages (common-law marriages) of Catholics as valid. At this council, the Church also defined marriage as one of the seven sacraments. This differed from Luther and Calvin, who denied marriage's sacramentality.

In the following centuries, the theology of marriage continued to develop. The 1917 *Code of Canon Law* viewed marriage as a contract between a man and a woman that could be broken only by death.

Vatican II dropped the distinction between the primary and secondary ends (purposes) of marriage (the procreation and the education of children were considered primary and the mutual love of spouses was considered secondary). The council said that the mutual love of the spouses and the procreation and education of children were in mutual relationship as co-equal ends of marriage. It also directed the development of a new *Rite of Marriage* that refocused Christian marriage in terms of a covenant rather than a contract. It said, "A marriage is established by the marriage covenant, the irrevocable consent that the spouses freely give to and receive from each other" (*Rite of Marriage* 2).

The revised *Code of Canon Law* (1983) describes marriage as a covenant between spouses. This reminds us of the covenant between God and Hebrew people and the covenant between Jesus and the Church. This code replaced the 1917 code that described marriage in terms of a contract, not a covenant.

Basic Church Teachings on Matrimony

Christian married couples are in a unique relationship. The sacrament of Matrimony presumes many
civil requirements of secular marriages (getting a
civil license, etc.) but adds more. As a sacrament,
it shares in the divine life of Christ and opens up a
deeper relationship with him through the couple's
love. Sacramental grace enables the husband and
wife to participate in God's love and creative activity by conceiving, bearing, and raising children. In so
doing, Jesus' presence continues among us.

Marriage is an essential part of God's plan. The
Catechism of the Catholic Church says, "Sacred Scripture begins with the creation of man and woman in
the image and likeness of God and concludes with a
vision of the 'wedding-feast of the Lamb' (Rev 19:7,
9; cf. Gen 1:26-27)" (CCC 1602).

Jesus showed marriage's dignity by his birth as a
human being. God chose Mary, his mother, to bring
the divine Son of God into the world, and Joseph, his
foster father, to be a devoted parent and husband.
Jesus also affirmed marriage's dignity at the wedding
feast of Cana (Jn 2:1-11).

As its author, God established laws that govern
marriage.[27] It exists for more than the couple or the
children, for marriage is the way the human race
continues. The Christian community depends on
marriage to pass on the faith that God entrusted to
the Church for our salvation.

The *Code of Canon Law* describes the matrimonial covenant, saying:

> The matrimonial covenant, by which a man and a woman establish between themselves a partnership of the whole of life and which is ordered by its nature to the good of the spouses and the procreation and education of offspring, has been raised by Christ the Lord to the dignity of a sacrament between the baptized. (CIC, c. 1055 §1)

Rooted in Baptism, Christian marriage is a covenant between a man and a woman for the whole of life. Yahweh's covenant with the Hebrew people prepared for the new and eternal covenant that Jesus entered into with his Church. Christian marriage is a covenant between spouses, reflecting Jesus' relationship with the Church. The mutual love of spouses reflects Jesus' love for the Church. As the *Catechism of the Catholic Church* says, "[T]heir mutual love becomes an image of the absolute and unfailing love with which God loves man" (CCC 1604). St. Paul views Christ's love for the Church in terms of marital love.

The unbroken covenant of Christ and the Church is linked with the unbroken covenant of married couples with each other. The Gospel of Matthew says that "what God has joined together, let no one separate" (Mt 19:6). The Church strongly affirms the indissolubility of Christian marriage and accepts every marriage, validly entered into by baptized persons, as a sacrament, whether the spouses are Catholic or not.

Rooted in a matrimonial covenant between the spouses, marriage takes place through the mutual consent of the spouses, who are the proper ministers of this sacrament. When two baptized persons marry in accordance with Church law, it is a sacramental marriage. Jesus raised the marital covenant of baptized persons to the dignity of a sacrament. Hence, "a valid matrimonial contract cannot exist between the baptized without it being by that fact a sacrament" (CIC, c. 1055 §2).

Christian marriages are signs, or sacraments, of the covenant between Christ and the Church (CCC 1617). Marriages between baptized and non-baptized persons, free to marry, are true marriages, but not sacramental ones. They do not share in the covenant relationship between Christ and his Church, but God also blesses them.

A bishop, priest, deacon, minister, or civil magistrate at non-Catholic marriages officiates and declares the couple "married." The couple's consent must be given before two witnesses. Marriages in the Catholic Church generally take place at a Mass or in a Liturgy of the Word apart from Mass. The ordained cleric (for example, a priest) is the Church's official witness in whose presence the man and woman exchange their mutual consent.

A marriage between a Catholic and a non-Catholic is commonly called a "mixed marriage." Mixed marriages can take place in the Catholic parish or the church of the non-Catholic partner with the Protestant minister officiating, with prior permission of the bishop of the Catholic party. To be a valid marriage, both partners must be free to marry in the Catholic Church and must freely and without any conditions exchange their consent. The couple must have no prior marital impediments and follow the Church's law.

Matrimony and Basic Human Needs

Matrimony helps a couple satisfy the basic human needs for love and companionship. After Adam and Eve's fall from grace, humans found themselves lonely and alienated from God. Feelings of separation imply the need for unity. Adam's fall from grace did not destroy this desire but intensified it. The need for unity comes from God, who created us. As Genesis 2:18 says, "It is not good that the man should be alone; I will make him a helper as his partner." Springing from this need for unity, the attraction between a man and a woman prepares the couple for marriage. It helps them satisfy the alienation caused by original sin.

The need for oneness with others is a built-in reason why we need community. Among various human groupings, the most intimate one is marriage and family life. Hence, Vatican II described marriage as an "intimate community of life and love" (CCC 1603). Jesus gave us the sacrament of Matrimony to help overcome loneliness and to fulfill marital responsibilities.

These responsibilities include begetting and raising children. As indicated above, the marriage covenant is "ordered by its nature to the good of the spouses and the procreation and education of offspring" (CIC, c. 1055 §1). The Church teaches that God put into men and women the natural desire to have children. This is not an add-on to marriage, not something to be accepted or dispelled at random, but an essential aspect, along with spousal love.

The need for permanency in marriage is bound up with the need for lasting spousal unity to insure the necessary bonding between spouses and their children.

ॐ

COMMUNAL AND PERSONAL IMPLICATIONS

In God' plan, marriage is a calling, a vocation. Accepting this call requires careful consideration. For this reason, the Church increasingly emphasizes the need for more preparation before marriage. With the allurements and attractions of contemporary society all around us, it's easy to approach Christian marriage more as a secular event than the beginning of a new spiritual way of living.

Christian marriages are fraught with challenges. The secular attraction of elaborate weddings often puts their religious aspect in a secondary place. This shows itself in the cost of the reception, wedding dress, flowers, and sundries. When overdone, the wedding preparation and the wedding itself become more show and style than substance.

Marriage is an important time for a couple to renew their commitment to Jesus and to their faith, and to ask for God's help. If they do not attend or fully participate at Mass regularly, they can begin doing so. It's also a valuable time for the couple to recognize how much marriage influences a child's faith and to make a commitment to raise their children in the faith. This may require a change in spousal attitudes toward Sunday as the Lord's Day and toward praying daily.

Discussing religion with each other and with family members is important for interfaith couples, who face pressures from parents, especially over their children's faith. Wishing to avoid conflicts over their children's Baptism and religious formation, many interfaith couples avoid the issue and do nothing. This has negative consequences for children.

Just as Christ remains faithful to his Church and does not abandon it, so married couples must remain faithful to each other. They must commit themselves to a loving relationship and to their family's spiritual well-being. If not, they cannot fulfill their responsibilities to love each other and raise a loving, faithful family. Infidelity shatters family bonds, breaks the trust required by the marital covenant, and exposes children to scandal, insecurity, and distorted attitudes.

God's grace, received in the sacrament of Matrimony, helps the couple to grow in love for each other and to strengthen their marriage for the ups and downs of married life. These marital graces help them fulfill their responsibilities to each other, their children, and their wider life. Cooperating with these graces moves the couple along their journey to eternal life.

Marriage is an important life transition that opens up the couple to new possibilities. As a rite of passage, it can start the couple on a new road to spiritual maturity.

With this in mind, take a few moments to consider the above comments on marriage or those listed below:

- Discuss the permanence, or indissolubility, of the marriage bond and talk about the contemporary challenges to the permanency of marriage. What are the implications for your life?

- How can a couple enhance their children's faith growth and religious formation?
- If you are married, how can this chapter help you have a happier, more successful marriage?
- When someone is considering marriage or engagement, what can you tell him or her about having a happy marriage? What is the spiritual component of your advice?
- While maintaining one's self-identity and respect, Christian marriage is a sacrament that involves full cooperation with the other person that draws its inspiration from Jesus' love and the sacrifice of himself on the cross. It's the opposite of self-gratification and involves the offering of oneself for a spouse and children. What does this mean to you?
- If feasible, how can we help lapsed Catholics (those whom we know) reconnect with the Church, as they prepare for marriage?
- It's often easier to see marriage more as a secular event than as a spiritual way of living with a partner committed to similar values. What does this say about the

need to select the right marriage partner and the need for family prayer, for
creating a Catholic home environment,
for weekly Mass attendance, and for frequent reception of Holy Communion?

- Christian service draws its inspiration
from Jesus' love, as manifested by his
death on the cross. How is this fruitfully
lived out in marriage?

- What does the following statement
mean to you: Christian marriage shares
in the divine life of Christ and opens up
a deeper level of relationship with him
through the love of the Christian couple.
It enables them to share in God's creative
activity by conceiving, bearing, and raising children.

- The sacrament of Matrimony is a gateway
affirming the sacramentality of the body
and God's love reflected through spousal
love. What does this imply as regards the
sacredness of your body and those of others, whether married or single?

જી

CHAPTER EIGHT

୬

Holy Orders

*Gateway to Deeper Incorporation Into
the Priesthood of Jesus Christ and
to Leadership in the Church*

THE SUN SPARKLED THROUGH THE TREES lining the
sidewalk, as I walked home one spring afternoon. I
was in my junior year of high school, and I had just
finished tennis practice. As I gazed at the sun's rays
coming through the large branches, I heard a voice
deep within me say, "God has something important
for you to do with your life." That's all it said. It didn't
say anything about going to college or the seminary,
but I wondered, "What is this important thing?"

I still wasn't sure what I wanted to do after gradu-
ation from high school. When I received a full scholarship to a Catholic university, I hesitated to accept
it, telling my parents that I was thinking of being a
priest. They said it was up to me.

A week later, my father arranged for us (him,
my mom, and me) to meet with our pastor. We dis-
cussed whether I should take the scholarship or go to

the seminary. After the pastor encouraged me to take the scholarship, I still hesitated.

The next week, I spoke to the university dean, who consulted with the school's president and board of trustees. They allowed me to put off the scholarship for a year, while I tried out the seminary.

I entered the seminary in the fall of 1952, but I did not like it. I did not connect with the lifestyle and prayer routine. The required courses were not the ones that I would have selected at the university. I longed to be outside the seminary grounds, to see my family, to attend sporting events, to have fun with friends, and to talk to them on the phone. I could do none of these and thought of leaving many times.

The year passed slowly. As it ended, I had to decide whether to stay there or leave and accept the scholarship. My feelings told me to leave, return to my previous lifestyle, and take the scholarship. But something deeper said, "No. Stay where you are." So I stayed. In retrospect, I never seriously considered leaving, even though I didn't enjoy seminary life. A force far greater than me carried me along.

As the seminary years went on, even though I did very well in class, I kept asking myself, "Am I really called to be a priest?" I never liked the seminary. As my preparation came to an end, I had to decide about being ordained.

While pondering this matter, the rector told me that the faculty and students selected me to be ordained a year early, to be a student prefect for the following year. Instead of fifteen more months, I had three months to decide. Something deep within me again urged me to say yes. I was ordained on August 15, 1959.

Uncertain seminary years prepared me for the changes in the Church after ordination. God sustained me through my doubts, fears, and good and bad times. Over the years, I've trusted the Holy Spirit within me for guidance in the ups and downs of priestly life, knowing that my vocation is deeper than I will ever imagine.

Today's seminaries are more open and welcoming, and they aim at developing well-rounded priests. Even so, challenges still exist, offering seminarians the opportunity to put themselves in God's hands.

Why did I begin this chapter on Holy Orders with my story? Perhaps because it can tell us that God's calling doesn't always follow what immediately pleases us. His ways of doing things are not always our ways. We are not the masters of our fate.

Seminary preparation readied me for unknown blessings and responsibilities that I never realized on ordination day. On that August morning, over fifty years ago, I accepted a new and never-ending life path, centered on a call to service and the desire to do something more for others.

Ordination is the gateway to Church leadership, as the one ordained shares Christ's words and sacraments with the Christian faithful. Bishops, priests, and deacons are to be symbols of the Christian life that all baptized Christians are to live. They are to follow Christ as personal, accessible, and humble servants.

Holy Orders as a Gateway

The sacrament of Holy Orders is the gateway to Church leadership through the sharing of Christ's words and sacraments with the Christian faithful by following Christ in a life of service. Without the leadership of ordained ministers, where would the Church be? Based on Jesus as its foundation, the Church continues to grow. Holy Orders is the gateway to special leadership roles, as the ordained minister shares God's saving graces through his ministry of Word, sacrament, and service. Holy Orders entrusts men with the leadership roles first given to Peter, the apostles, and their successors.

Each different order (bishop, priest, or deacon) gives the ordained man greater responsibilities. Bishops, who are the successors of the apostles, act in union with the pope, the successor of St. Peter, to rule, guide, and shepherd Christ's Church. Priests assist them, as do deacons.

The Church assigns specific functions to bishops, priests, and deacons that no other Church ministers perform. Through their leadership, the Church fulfills her responsibility to teach, to rule, and to sanctify.

They set directions for the rest of the Church. Although vowed religious women, brothers, and members of the lay faithful exercise leadership roles, the primary leadership roles rest with the clergy.

History of Holy Orders

The sacrament of Holy Orders includes the orders of bishop, presbyter (priest), and deacon.

In the Old Testament, God selected the Jews, his Chosen People, and made them "a priestly kingdom and a holy nation" (Ex 19:6). Among the twelve tribes, Yahweh singled out the tribe of Levi to perform liturgical services, often centering on offering sacrifices in atonement for people's sins. The Levitical priesthood was connected with serving in the sanctuary. Priests received no land but specialized in priestly jobs, like offering bloody sacrifices to God.

In contrast to such bloody sacrifices, Genesis describes an occasion when Abraham, returning from battle, met Melchizedek, king of Salem and priest of the most high God (Gen 14:18-20). Not of the tribe of Levi, Melchizedek offered gifts of bread and wine to God.

The New Testament refers to Melchizedek as being "Without father, without mother, without genealogy, having neither beginning of days nor end of life, but resembling the Son of God, he remains a priest forever" (Heb 7:3). Speaking of Christ, the

Letter to the Hebrews says this: "Now if perfection had been attainable through the levitical priesthood . . . what further need would there have been to speak of another priest arising according to the order of Melchizedek, rather than one according to the order of Aaron?" (Heb 7:11; Aaron is considered as the model for Jewish high priests).

Christ fulfilled the passage about Melchizedek quoted in the Psalms: "You are a priest forever according to the order of Melchizedek" (Ps 110:4). Melchizedek's unbloody sacrifice of bread and wine prefigured Jesus' offering at the Last Supper and his priesthood (Gen 14:18-20). The ordination ceremony of a priest repeats the words of this psalm, reminding him that he serves according to the order of Melchizedek.

The New Testament disassociated Jesus from the bloody sacrifices of the Temple. He never called himself a priest, although he performed priestly functions, especially offering his life as a sacrifice for sins and giving us the Eucharist as a perpetual reminder of his love.

At the Last Supper, after giving the disciples his body and blood, Jesus commanded them to "do this in remembrance of me" (Lk 22:19). Ordained bishops and priests, following in the footsteps of the apostles and their successors, continue to carry out his command.

The Letter to the Hebrews refers to Jesus as the "great high priest" (Heb 4:14) and makes clear that his priesthood is unlike the priesthood of the Old Law. He is the only priest, contrasted to many priests in the Old Testament. He sacrificed his life on the cross as the Paschal Lamb, and he is the High Priest who offers himself to the Father as a ransom for sins. With Jesus as head of the Church, the early community of believers regarded themselves as a priestly people.

Jesus left us no organized blueprint for ordained ministry beyond that of Peter, the Twelve, and other ministers mentioned in New Testament writings. To meet the needs of the early Christians, different structures emerged in various local churches. Paul describes forms of charismatic ministry in the Church of Corinth, indicating that gifts of the Holy Spirit make possible the ministries of evangelists, prophets, pastors, teachers, and administrators. Churches with many converts from Judaism developed a ministerial structure similar to the Jewish synagogue service, with an *episcopos* (overseer, or bishop), who presided over a council of seventy presbyters (elders, or priests).

After Christianity separated from Judaism, Lawrence Mick explains that "the bishop was seen more and more as the new high priest presiding over the Eucharistic celebration of Christ's sacrifice."[28] The "monarchial bishop" (one bishop in charge, under whom the presbyters and deacons ministered) was established by the end of the first century, largely because the Christian community needed one clear source of authority to witness to and teach the authentic message of Christ and the apostles. The monarchial bishop emerged largely because heresies and factions in the Church (especially Gnosticism, which denied the full humanity of Jesus, teaching that his divinity is covered over by his cloak of humanity) threatened to tear apart the Church's unity.

By the end of the first century, the orders of *episcopos* (overseer, or bishop), *presbyteros* (elder, or priest) and *diaconos* (deacon) are clear. Deacons assisted bishops in their ministry for several centuries. When presbyters became assistants of bishops, the order of the deacon as a distinct ministry ceased, not to be restored until the Second Vatican Council.

Long before the Middle Ages began, the Church had already given priests the authority to celebrate the Eucharist, preach, and administer the sacraments. The Protestant Reformation rejected the pope's authority and questioned many aspects of clerical authority. The Council of Trent countered this challenge and clarified the role of the ordained and non-ordained Church members. Its teachings remained the norm until Vatican II.

Vatican II revised the rite of ordination and restored the order of the diaconate. It expanded the laity's role and dropped the minor orders of porter and exorcist, kept the orders of lector (reader) and acolyte (server), and dropped the major order of the subdiaconate. The recognition that Baptism makes the recipient a member of the common priesthood and the clarification of how it relates to the ministerial priesthood received at ordination shifted the Church's perspective on Holy Orders and ministry. The clergy and laity participate in the one priesthood of Jesus Christ in different ways.

Vatican II spoke of the Church as the People of God. It authorized the clergy to act in unison with the baptized community, calling them forth to exercise the ministries that God entrusts to them as lay Church members.

The clergy's and laity's shifting roles initiated an explosion of ministries. New ones developed, including the ministries of pastoral or finance council member, liturgist, pastoral associate, catechetical leader, and faith-formation leader. Today, the lay faithful serve in these ministries alongside the priests and permanent deacons.

Basic Church Teachings on Holy Orders

The *Catechism of the Catholic Church* says this:

Holy Orders is the sacrament through which the mission entrusted by Christ to his apostles continues to be exercised in the Church until the end of time: thus it is the sacrament of apostolic ministry. It includes three degrees: episcopate, presbyterate, and diaconate. (CCC 1536)

In ancient Rome, a ruling body was called an *ordo*. In a Christian context, "ordination" was the process that incorporated a man into an *ordo* — most specifically into the episcopate, the presbyterate, or the diaconate. The Church's main orders are the orders of bishops, presbyters (priests), and deacons (CCC 1537). Ordination is the sacramental action that incorporates men into these orders.

The Decree on the Ministry and Life of Priests (*Presbyterorum Ordinis*) repeats the fundamental Catholic truth that the sacrament of Holy Orders sets ordained men apart, confers a special mark, or character, on them, and configures them "to Christ the priest in such a way that they are able to act in the person of Christ the head" (n. 2). The *Code of Canon Law* says, "A baptized male alone receives sacred ordination validly" (CIC, c. 1024). This means that in imitation of Christ and consistent with the history of the Catholic Church from the beginning, only baptized men may be validly ordained to Holy Orders.

Ordained priests and deacons assist in the ministry of bishops, the successors of the apostles. Priests assist them in celebrating the Eucharist, in administering the sacraments, in proclaiming God's Word, and in serving. To carry out their tasks, priests unite with the bishop to build up the Body of Christ through servant leadership.

Deacons assist bishops and priests "in the celebration of the divine mysteries, above all the Eucharist, in the distribution of Holy Communion, in assisting at and blessing marriages, in the proclamation of the Gospel and preaching, in presiding over funerals, and in dedicating themselves to the various ministries of charity" (CCC 1570). The deacon serves the community in various ways, administers the sacrament of Baptism, and officiates at marriages. The entire Church is under the leadership of the pope, the successor of St. Peter. He and the bishops united with him are the Church's supreme living, teaching authority, which we call the "Magisterium."

There is only one priesthood in the New Covenant — namely, the priesthood of Jesus Christ. All baptized persons share in Christ's priesthood. The common priesthood of the baptized and the ministerial priesthood of the ordained participate differently in Christ's one priesthood. Although both the common and ministerial priesthood share in Jesus' priesthood, a real, essential, qualitative difference exists between them. Both Baptism and Holy Orders place their own unique, indelible seal on the recipient. The baptismal seal forever marks the baptized person as a follower of Christ, and the seal of Holy Orders forever marks the ordained man as a servant leader in the Church, acting in the person of Christ.

Holy Orders cannot be repeated. It gives priests the graces necessary to fulfill their roles, as the Holy Spirit inspires, guides, and supports them in their ministry.

Common features exist in the ordination rite of bishops, priests, and deacons. The necessary and essential elements in the sacrament of Holy Orders in all its degrees include the bishop imposing his hands on the head of the one being ordained and reciting the special consecratory prayer. In this prayer, the bishop asks God to pour his Holy Spirit on the one being ordained and to give him the necessary gifts to assist him in fulfilling the order to which he is ordained (CCC 1573).

In the Latin Catholic Church, only celibate, baptized men can be ordained as priests or bishops. Celibacy is a powerful symbol of the kingdom of God, in imitation of Jesus, who was celibate. In giving themselves in this way to Christ, whom they imitate as servant leaders of the Church, they bear a unique witness to the Risen Lord in their commitment to God's people. Married men can be ordained as deacons, but if their wives die, they must remain celibate. Some Eastern Catholic Churches allow married men to be ordained priests. The bishop is always the minister of the sacrament of Holy Orders.

The priest's most eminent role happens when he presides at the liturgy, especially the Eucharist. The priest represents Christ. In the liturgy, the Risen Lord comes among us sacramentally through the words and actions of the priest, and shares again the fruits of his Paschal Mystery. As the servant leader of the community, the priest-presider at Mass is a symbol of service for the entire congregation, challenging the faithful to grow in faith and to become what they are called to be as servants in imitation of Christ.

As the community leader, the pastor is his parish's chief catechist and liturgist. Other catechetical and liturgical ministers assist him, as do parents, who are their children's first catechists and liturgists. A pastor's responsibility includes developing catechesis on all levels and supporting parish liturgical endeavors. He is obliged to maintain authentic Catholic teaching and solid liturgical celebrations. A holy pastor influences those being catechized, fosters the liturgy, and encourages the faithful to grow in faith. He is a symbol of Christ, who lived, celebrated, suffered, and died so that we might rise with him to eternal glory.

Holy Orders and Basic Human Needs

We have a basic need to care for others and to look for good leaders to help this happen. Leadership roles in our family, Church, and elsewhere address this need. In the Church, this responsibility belongs primarily to ordained ministers.

Jesus gave us the sacrament of Holy Orders to raise up Church leaders who will help us to know God's will, to share his graces, and to fulfill our Christian responsibilities. To effectively carry out their ministry, ordained ministers need affirmation and support. Just as the clergy are to let the faithful know they have value as sons and daughters of God, so also clerics need support from the laity.

The ordained minister's life of service cannot be self-centered. Jesus is the model. As a person for others, Jesus attracted others to himself because he was a servant leader. He is the perfect model for ordained ministers.

Jesus' great love (called "agape love") inspired early Christians, as they realized that his suffering and death atoned for their sins and won back favor from God. After Pentecost, the apostles left their homes and traveled to the ends of the earth, to proclaim Jesus' message and to celebrate his presence in the sacraments.

Ordained ministers follow in Jesus' footsteps. He invites them to a life of self-service, as they reach out to the poor, the forgotten, and the downtrodden. In so doing, they fulfill their ministry in imitation of him, who is "the way, and the truth, and the life" (Jn 14:6).

ഏ

COMMUNAL AND PERSONAL IMPLICATIONS

What kind of clerical leaders do parishioners want? The laity look for sensitive clerical leaders to help them during difficult times. Such leaders stop what they are doing to minister to a dying person, to reach out to the troubled, and to counsel the doubtful. They may not know all the answers, but they respect those who ask. They are good listeners, open to the movements of the Holy Spirit. The laity seek out such leaders as models of Christian living. Parish communities need humble, holy bishops and priests as models to follow.

The Christian community wants the clergy to accurately and completely proclaim Christ's message so that they can better understand their responsibilities and respond by reaching out to those in need. At times, the laity expect them to challenge individuals and social institutions to act justly and with charity. The clergy respond by making service a part of their lives.

The laity want ordained ministers to act with professionalism and humble dignity. This is enhanced when the clergy remember that the sacraments are for the people and do not place needless burdens on them. They realize that coming to faith and growing in faith are a gradual process, and that grace works differently in every person. They remind their staff and parishioners that God dictates the agenda, not them. They encourage all parishioners to pray for and persevere with family members and friends who have left active participation in the Catholic community.

Parishioners look for the wisdom in ordained ministers that moves them to work with those whose faith is weak, to strengthen that faith, and to support them when they desire to have their child baptized or to get married in a Catholic ceremony. Rites of passage like these provide opportunities to help the larger community recognize that people are at different stages of faith and to encourage parishioners to see the journey of faith as a movement toward mature faith. Parishes need clerical leaders to preside at liturgical celebrations with faith and devotion. In short, parishioners expect their clerical leaders to act in the person of Christ.

With this in mind, take a few moments to reflect on the above comments on Holy Orders or on those listed below:

- What qualities do the best priests you know possess?
- What qualities do you prefer in your pastor and those who serve your parish?
- If you had your choice for a pastor, who would you primarily prefer, a pastoral priest or a good administrator?
- If your son, relative, or friend were interested in becoming a priest, would you foster and encourage his calling? Why or why not? If you answer yes, how would you do this?
- How can you support priests in their ministry? What support do they need today?

To what degree do you feel that priests are appreciated for their ministry?

- In what ways can we all help priests be better servant leaders of our parishes in imitation of Christ?

- Ordained ministers let the laity know that they are important participants in God's plan of salvation. They do so as community leaders, calling the entire parish to more. To what degree do you see this happening in your parish? What can you do to make it better?

- Baptism makes a person a member of the common priesthood, related to the ministerial priesthood received at ordination. What are the consequences of this for the involvement of the laity in the Church's life, especially in their families and in evangelization?

- The Latin Catholic Church permits only celibate, baptized males to be ordained priests and bishops. Some Eastern Catholic Churches allow married men to be ordained to the priesthood. How do you feel about the differences in the Latin and Eastern Catholic Churches on this matter, and which do you prefer? What are practical consequences that follow from each tradition, as regards clerical relationships, family life, and other issues?

CONCLUSION

WHEN I WAS A LITTLE BOY, I'd sit on our front steps, across the street from St. William's Church, and watch people coming to and leaving Mass and other services. I thought, "Something important must be going on there." They came early in the morning, in the afternoon, in the evening, and sometimes at night. As I grew older, I wondered what the procession that went up and down our street on the day called "Corpus Christi" (Body of Christ) had to do with the people often going to church.

Each time something new happened at church I asked Dad and Mom. They answered in ways that a young boy could understand. Sometimes, though, they mentioned the word "sacrament," which was too deep for me. When I began school at age six, I learned that the sacraments are part of my life. They are about God the Father, Jesus, and the Holy Spirit.

A year later, I received First Holy Communion. Our schoolteacher taught us how to ask for God's pardon in confession. Soon afterward, I went to my aunt's wedding and my uncle's funeral. I thought, "Wow, these sacraments are special. The Church has something important for everyone!"

As I grew older, I learned more about the sacraments. One day, I felt called to share these sacraments with others, so I entered the seminary. Eventually, ordination made this possible, and fifty years later I still do the same thing.

Much of my story is similar to that of my grade- and high-school classmates, except that they chose to marry and raise children to carry on our Catholic faith tradition with their children. The sacraments play a central role throughout all of our lives — so much so, that when we assemble for a class reunion, my classmates first see if the church is available for celebrating Mass, and then they ask me to celebrate it with them.

As we come to appreciate the sacraments more, may we realize how blessed we are to be able to share in this precious treasure of the sacraments, given by Jesus himself, when he lived and walked among us!

Throughout this book I have emphasized the importance of celebrating the sacraments as gateways to God. We celebrate them throughout our lives. In *Baptism*, Jesus' life-giving waters invite us into a new and special relationship with God. We are transformed and become new persons, children of God and heirs of eternal happiness. *Confirmation* strengthens our calling to follow Christ and gives us graces to sustain us during difficult life experiences. The *Eucharist* opens up a deeper appreciation of God's presence in worship and life. Jesus' real presence in this sacrament reflects God's presence everywhere, and it invites us to enter through the mystery of Jesus' body and blood into a new world, suffused with God.

Through the gateway of *Reconciliation*, we experience God's love, mercy, and forgiveness, reflected in Jesus' suffering and death on the cross to atone for our sins. This gateway helps us, regardless of our sins, to recognize that God's mercy is open to all sinners. The *Anointing of the Sick* is the gateway to healing in this life and eternal happiness in the next, when tragedy strikes or we are wearied by sickness and old age.

Matrimony sacramentalizes God's love for us, symbolized in the mutual love of a man and a woman. This gateway unlocks untold blessings for the spouses, and it invites them to love each other as Christ loves us and to raise their children according to God's designs. Marital love is a gateway to a better understanding of the deep love that God has for us. *Holy Orders* is the gateway to leadership and service in the Church as ordained ministers.

My prayer is that this book will help us to better appreciate the sacraments as gateways to God and to see more clearly how they can motivate our lives. May the sacraments lead us to a happier life here and to eternal blessedness hereafter.

NOTES

1. A series of General Audiences, beginning September 5, 1979, and ending November 28, 1984.
2. *New Baltimore Catechism* No. 3, Connell Edition, Lesson 23, n. 304.
3. Papal Audience (February 20, 1980), *L'Osservatore Romano* (February 25, 1980), p. 1.
4. Ibid.
5. Pope St. Leo the Great (Sermon 51, 3–4. 8), *Liturgy of the Hours*, Office of Readings, Second Reading, Second Sunday of Lent.
6. Ibid.
7. *Gaudium et Spes* (Pastoral Constitution on the Church in the Modern World) 22. Cf. also *Lumen Gentium* (Dogmatic Constitution on the Church) 16 and *Ad Gentes Divinitus* (Decree on the Church's Missionary Activity) 7.
8. *Unitatis Redintegratio* (Decree on Ecumenism) 22.
9. Lawrence E. Mick, *Understanding the Sacraments Today* (Collegeville, MN: Liturgical Press, 1987), p. 44.
10. Ibid., p. 45.
11. *Lumen Gentium* (Dogmatic Constitution on the Church) 11.
12. Thomas Bokenkotter, *Dynamic Catholicism* (New York: Doubleday, 1992), p. 206.

13. Council of Trent (1551), DS 1651. Cf. CCC 1374.

14. Sacred Congregation of Rites, *Instruction on Eucharistic Worship* 9.

15. CCC 1436 quotes the Council of Trent (1551), DS 1638: "It [the Eucharist] is a remedy to free us from our daily faults and to preserve us from mortal sins."

16. Annemarie S. Kidder, *Making Confession, Hearing Confession: A History of the Cure of Souls* (Collegeville, MN: Liturgical Press, 2010), p. 6.

17. Cf. St. Pacian, *Liturgy of the Hours*, Office of Readings, Second Reading, Friday and Saturday, Nineteenth Week in Ordinary Time.

18. Bokenkotter, p. 222.

19. Ibid.

20. Ibid.

21. Mick, p. 95.

22. Ibid., p. 97.

23. *Lumen Gentium* (Dogmatic Constitution on the Church) 11.

24. Sess. 14 *De Extrema Unctione*, cap. 2CT 7, 1, 356; Dens-Schon, 1696.

25. *Pastoral Care of the Sick: Rites of Anointing and Viaticum* 25.

26. Mick, p. 114.

27. *Gaudium et Spes* (Pastoral Constitution on the Church in the Modern World) 48.

28. Mick, p. 134.